James Howell

A Tale of the Sea, Sonnets

And other Poems

James Howell

A Tale of the Sea, Sonnets
And other Poems

ISBN/EAN: 9783337074630

Printed in Europe, USA, Canada, Australia, Japan

Cover: Foto ©ninafisch / pixelio.de

More available books at **www.hansebooks.com**

A TALE OF THE SEA,

SONNETS,

AND OTHER POEMS.

BY
JAMES HOWELL.

TO

SIR J. CORDY BURROWS,

W. M. HOLLIS, J. J. SEWELL, AND H. WILLETT, Esqrs.,

THIS VOLUME IS DEDICATED

WITH FEELINGS OF THE HIGHEST ESTEEM,

BY

THEIR GRATEFUL AND OBEDIENT SERVANT,

JAMES HOWELL.

BRIGHTON,
    56, CLARENCE SQUARE,
        September, 1873.

CONTENTS.

	PAGE
Song	1
To a Field Daisy	3
The Minstrel	5
A Tale of the Sea :—	
Dedication	11
Part I.—Prelude	12
The Tale	16
Part II	27
Part III.—Prelude. Boyhood Reminiscences	40
Rhoda Marten	56
A Day Dream	57
Autumn	65
The Dying Maiden	67
A Love Letter	72
Lines on the Opening of the Brighton Working Men's Institute	76
Spring Time	78
Soul Embodiments	81
To Arthur Sienkiewicz, Esq.	84
Sonnets Composed in 1859 :—	
On the Rev. F. W. Robertson, M.A.	89
England	90

Contents.

Sonnets composed in 1859 (*continued*):— PAGE
  Beachy Head ... 92
  Brighton ... 92
  Goldstone Bottom ... 93
  The South Downs ... 94
  A Life Phase ... 95

Sonnets and Poems composed in 1860:—
  Progression ... 97
  Charles Sienkiewicz, the Polish Poet and Historian ... 98
  Seaford ... 99
  Love of Nature ... 102
  To Some Early Violets ... 102
  The Dyke ... 103
  A Plea for the Poor ... 104
  Lines written in a Field before the House in which my Father Died ... 106
  Mary ... 109
  Love-Song ... 111
  Helen ... 114
  The Seasons:—
    Spring ... 117
    Summer ... 117
    Autumn ... 118
    Winter ... 119
  Rosa ... 120
  God's Pioneers ... 122
  Independence ... 123
  Written during a Severe Illness ... 124
  A Christian Gentleman ... 125

Contents.

Sonnets and Poems composed in 1860 (*continued*) :-

	PAGE
To Mark Anthony Lower, Esq., F.S.A.	126
May	127
A South-Down Sketch	130
Morning	132
To Wentworth Holworthy, Esq.	133
Christmas Eve	135
The Sea	136
To the Working-Men of Brighton	138
To Gold Worshippers	138
Brighton Race Hill	139

Sonnets and Poems written in 1861 :—

To John Robertson, Esq.	142
Country Longings	143
Life's Autumn	143
Hastings	144
Written under great Mental Affliction	147
The Mew's-Nest Seeker	149

Songs written in 1862 :—

Lily Bella	152
Jeanette	153
Emma	155
Minnie	156
Winnie	157
Jenny	159

Sonnets and Poems written in 1868 :—

Wail of a Bruised Spirit	160
Epistle to Mark Antony Lower, Esq., M.A., F.S.A.	161
To W. C. T., Esq., on the Death of his Beloved Wife	164

Sonnet, Songs, and Poems written in 1870, 1871, and 1873 :— PAGE

On the Death of a Thrush 168
Sweet Seventeen 169
Lucy Green 170
Esther 172
Almena Vaughan 173
A Song for the Times 175
The Poet's Love-Song... 177
Elise 179
A Tear for the Poor Old Maids 181
The Ocean of Love 182
To Mr. Napper 184
Annie Kent 186
Amy 189
May-Song 192
A Walking Barometer... 194
Epitaph 197
Waif-Thoughts 199

A TALE OF THE SEA,

SONNETS, AND OTHER POEMS.

SONG.

1836.

THOU land of my fathers ! thou land of the brave !
Encircled by foam-wreath of blue-dashing wave,
Cloud-crested, rock-founded, majestic, and free,
Thou'rt set like a gem in the midst of the sea.

Thou land of my fathers ! thy beautiful bowers,
Thy hills and thy valleys are studded with flowers ;
Let Greece or Italia some fond heart inspire,
I love thee, sweet land of the rose and the brier.

B

Song.

Thou land of my fathers! thy soil has been trod
By heroes who've bled for their country and God,
By bards who have sung of their deeds unto thee,
Sweet home of the exile, the brave, and the free.

Thou land of my fathers! while life kindles here,
To thy mem'ry I'll cling, thy white shores revere;
And when my rapt spirit takes flight from the earth,
'Twill watch o'er thy welfare, sweet land of my birth.

TO A FIELD DAISY,

ON SEEING IT CLOSE ON THE APPROACH OF A STORM.

1839.

Low droops thy tiny head, my pretty flower,
   As thou dost gather in thy globe-like form,
Unable to resist the power
     Of the approaching storm.

Thy silver fringe, expanded on the plain,
   Was lovely to the eye, thou fairy thing!
Why dost thou tremble at the rain,
     And hide thy blossoming?

Does some bright spirit 'bide within thy cell—
   Some fairy reveller of the starry sky—
Who oft sports gaily in the dell,
     Unseen to mortal eye?

Scarce did the windows of the golden sun
   His spangled rays of light upon thee shed,
Than thou didst wake, belovèd one!
     And raise thy little head.

To a Field Daisy.

Now thou art closed, and mournful to the sight,
    Drooping thy crimson head, weighed down with tears,
Like a poor melancholy wight,
        O'erburdened with his years.

But cheer thee, pretty one, for when the storm
    That hovers o'er thee, has but passed away,
Again thy tiny, fragile form,
        Will open to the day.

Our pleasures and our pains are mixed together;
    Sorrow and joy o'er each exert their power:
We both are subject to the weather,
        Weak, drooping flower!

Life has its changes: every plant that grows
    Is sometimes painèd by the earth's dull breath:
It springs, it flourishes, and blows,
        And, like man, meets with death!

———o———

THE MINSTREL.

1840.

An aged minstrel, barely clad,
    And pale and wan was he,
Awoke his harp to strains of wo
    Beneath a shady tree.

His notes were plaintive, and his song
    Was made of simplest words;
And did that minstrel tell his tale
    Alone to forest-birds?

Oh, no; beside him beauty sat,
    A peerless lady bright,
As lovely as the spotless rose,
    All clad in garments white.

She cheered the minstrel with a smile,
    As sweet as beauteous May;
He threw aside his snowy locks,
    And thus began his lay:

"Ah! I was bred in lordly halls,
　Where wealth its power displays;
Caressed by all, in Fortune's lap
　I passed my childhood days.

"My infant limbs were clad in robes,
　Embroidered rich with gold;
And bright and happy days were passed,
　Which now are dark and cold.

"At Tewkesbury my father fell
　For the bonny proud red rose;
And when the white was crimsoned o'er
　Stern Fortune dealt her blows.

"Our lands were seized by cruel York,
　And I in durance thrown;
Till wily Gloucester set me free
　With but this harp my own.

"In youth I loved a lady fair,
　Whose feelings were refined
By witching strains of poesy,
　Those gold-thoughts of the mind.

"I sought her, but I found her not
    Till many years passed by;
So, friendless, homeless, 'twas my lot
    To live by minstrelsy.

"I travelled far o'er many lands,
    A woful time had I;
And prayed for death to end my woes,
    But yet I could not die!

"E'er haunted by a spectral form,
    Pale as the light of stars,
Pale as the corpses that had fallen
    In England's bloody wars!

"Where'er I went this spectre went,
    Which way I turned did go;
It led me to my native land,
    Where blood had ceased to flow.

"I passed the place, a lovely spot,
    Which I shall ne'er forget;
Where first my own true love I saw—
    My fancy sees her yet!

"The lily and the sweet moss-rose
    Were rivals on her cheek;
Her form was cast in beauty's mould;
    Her temper sweetly meek.

"And there again I sang my song,
    As I now sing to thee;
And there again I saw my love;—
    My wild heart throbbed with glee.

"Though years had passed and left me poor,
    To me she still was true;
And tear-drops trickled down her cheeks
    Like beads of pearly dew!

"'I've sought thee, my belovèd one,
    From sunny morn till eve.
A bonny minstrel hast thou come,
    A lord thou didst me leave.'

"This said, she wept upon my breast,
    And we were happy then;
But happiness, alas! how short,
    And grief how long, to men!

"For cruel Death, so fair a form,
　Alas! he could not spare:
Too sweet, too exquisite a flower,
　For this bleak world of care!

"That pale, pale spectre laid his hand
　Upon my love so true;
The moss-rose faded from her cheeks,
　The lily whiter grew.

"He stamped upon that angel-face
　His death-seal—oh! my God!
I read Thy awful characters,
　And bowed beneath Thy rod.

"She died in these enfeebled arms,
　Her own did me enfold;
One parting look, one fond embrace;
　Oh, God!—her lips were cold!

"A sudden pain shot through my brain,
　Hot tears gushed from my eyes:
Then senseless on her corpse I fell,
　A grief-struck man to rise.

"They laid her forth within a shell;
  Placed in her hand sweet flowers,
The offspring of the plants which she
  Had set in childhood's hours.

"The green grass shimmered in the sun
  And rippled like the sea;
The wind shook dew from every flower
  That blossomed on the lea;

"When she was borne by six young maids,
  All on a green-bough bier;
And soon in cold, cold earth was laid
  The form I loved so dear!

"The birds sang sweetly o'er her grave,
  The flowers bloomed prettily;
Sweet lady! drop one tear for her,
  And, lady, pity me!"

A TALE OF THE SEA.

1840.

INSCRIBED TO THE MEMORY OF ALMENA ALETTA VAUGHAN,

WHO LEFT THIS WORLD JUNE 21ST, 1843.

To thy bright spirit, wise and virtuous maiden,
   I dedicate the simple lay which thou
Upon thy bed of suffering, sorrow-laden,
   Of old inspired. Oh, I remember how
Upon thy lily face sweet smiles alighted,
   At my rude essays in the art of rhyme,—
And as I progressed, how thou wert delighted,
   And praised and censured me from time to time !

Neat was thy sick room ; flowers blooming ever
   Perfumed the air ; books, flowers were to thee
Thy life, thy world, thy love ! With high endeavour
   Thou mad'st me read myself, my errors see.
When false friends flattered too, thy great devotion
   To truth and duty shunned the two-faced throng ;
Thy pity for my faults awoke emotion,
   And I did love thee, spirit of my song.

Ah! woe is me! What floods of grief are welling
  From my life's fountain, whilst I weep hot tears
For wronging thee. From thy celestial dwelling
  Come down, sweet spirit, and expel my fears;
In the mid watches of our mother's slumbers,
  At morning, noon, and evening, I have heard
Thy thoughtful whispering, in liquid numbers,
  Sweet as the melody of night's lone bird!

Be mine the task to catch th' exalted measure,
  And to infuse its spirit in my verse,
Which e'er to me has been a source of pleasure
  Mingled with pain, my blessing and my curse:
Thou art not dead! only from me divided
  By mystery's veil, that hides the Beulah-land;
Here, stern affliction o'er thy life presided;
  There, thou'rt healed by the Great Physician's hand!

PART I.

PRELUDE.

Low sinks the sun, and his gigantic shadows
  Sweep o'er the valley, while the lowing herd,

Released from labour, graze in fields and meadows;
  No warbler sings except the pretty bird,
Man's loved companion, who comes uninvited,
  Singing of spring, heedless of winter's scowl,
Pecks at our windows, with his crumbs delighted,
  Fearless of snow-fall, or the north wind's howl.

Robin! I love to hear thee, pretty fellow,
  At evening, perched upon a leafless spray,
When the gold corn is stacked and fields are yellow,
  Whistling with merry heart my griefs away.
When other birds have wandered o'er the ocean,
  When sap retreats, and leaves begin to fall,
Still warblest thou thy pious heart-devotion,
  Lifeful mid death, the happiest bird of all.

The changeful Earth was stripped of all her glory;
  Naked she sat, and wrung her hands in tears;
Sighing among old ruins her sad story,
  While spectre-haunted by a thousand fears.
Her voice was mournful in the ocean-surges,
  And most unmusical mid forests sighed,—
While autumn winds were mumbling solemn dirges,
  Amid their wailings she laid down and died.

Oh, sweetly rest upon thy snowy pillow.
    There is no death! 'Tis but a winter sleep;
Soon wilt thou rise, and like the tidal billow,
    Cause mind to flow, and out of green forms peep.
Rest, wearied spirit 'neath thy light shroud hoary.
    Winter will melt away before the spring,
And thou wilt walk the earth in hallowed glory,
    Soar in the air, and 'mid green copses sing.

On England's southern coast, a promontory
    Shoots from the sea-base up into the sky,
There has it stood for ages in its glory,
    Frowning on foaming billows rolling by.
Sad yawning grave of many a gallant vessel,
    Have been the waters of a neighbouring bay,
Where life and death engage in angry wrestle,
    On the world's verge, where gloams eternal day.

There, when the south-west wind is madly blowing,
    Snow-crested waves break with a thunder-roar;
The seamews scream, the tide is landward flowing,
    Breaks through the beach and inundates the shore.
Such was the case one day in bleak November,
    One thousand eight hundred and twenty-four:

The streets were rivers. Well do I remember
That awful sight. May it be seen no more!

For here and there, from out the water soaring,
   A solitary roof or chimney-top was seen,
And hap a human being wildly roaring
   Above the winds and waves for help. The Steyne
Was the chief roadstead, where boats came flying
   Upon the mighty wings of that wild blast,
And mid the dim of screaming, bawling, crying,
   Over the wooden rails their anchors cast

From its deep fount the crazy sea was gushing,
   Sweeping before it everything, like dust
Before the whirlwind! Onward it came, rushing
   Into the Poor House, where the stinted crust
Was handed round to many a poor old sinner,
   Who started up with hair erect, right glad
To run away for once without his dinner,
   And leave it to old Ocean, hunger-mad.

Away went haystack whirling and sailing,
   Its only mariner a poor old hen,
Clucking with fear mid waters round prevailing.
   Wishing herself in farmyard safe again.

Up, through the streets the uncurbed waves were roaring,
  Dashing in windows, flooding houses deep,
Driving the inmates, their sad fate deploring,
  Into the upper rooms to wail and weep.

How the town trembled when the storm swept over,
  Flapping his strong winds, making buildings shake,
Lashing the water-mass which then did cover
  Beamland and common, causing hearts to ache.
God stilled the wind! The sea retreated growling,
  In its trail leaving the envenomed breath
Of slaughtering Typhus, who walked forth scowling,
  Foot-tracked by madness and God's angel, Death.

THE TALE.

But to my tale. The fishermen are calling—
  Launching their little skiffs upon the sea;
While in the east, night's star-wrought veil is falling,
  And sheep go bleating fold-ward from the lea.
A fisher leaves the shore with carol merry,
  Unfurls the sail, and ploughs the trembling main,—
His farewell sings, "'Twill not be long, my Mary,
  Ere I with plenty shall return again."

A Tale of the Sea.

She rushes through the waves that sparkle brightly
    In the white ocean pathway left behind ;
Away she skims, a seamew winging lightly
    Over the billows, like a thing of mind.
Pale was the moon, a reddish halo round her
    As she came rising o'er the eastern hill ;
Sweet Polly stood,—love's mighty spell had bound her,
    A statue there !   Sky, earth, and sea, were still.

She stood upon the beach, from which her lover
    Had just departed, and her heart beat wild,
The stars seemed reeling in the heavens above her,—
    Before her lay heaving like new-weaned child
In an unquiet slumber, the great ocean,
    For solemn noises rumbled in the air.
With grief-clasped hands, the maiden with emotion
    Said, in sad tones, " I would he were not there."

Then quickly hastened to her humble dwelling,
    Built by the cliffs that frowned upon the sea,—
The lashing winds the angry waves were swelling,
    Dashing them shoreward with velocity.
There by the cottage door she stood suppressing
    A flood of feeling, drying up her tears,

Till a dame showered on her head a blessing,
    And then beneath a smile she hid her fears.

The lightning flashed, and the sky-rending thunder
    Came booming on a sudden gust of wind,
The welkin rang and seemed to burst asunder
    The vaulted dome, and stun the human mind.
Then all was still again, except the roaring
    Of foaming billows breaking on the strand.
Poor Polly raised her hands to heaven, imploring
    That her dear Charles might safely reach the land.

The south was beautiful as morn, when beaming
    In all her radiant glory from the sea,
For forkèd fire-flames from the clouds were streaming,
    Tinging their purple edges goldenly !
Some ran like spirits with ethereal lightness
    'Long the sea's surface, dancing on the spray;
The windows of the heavens reflected brightness,
    And earth became that night as light as day !

Could Polly stay within her habitation,
    Weeping and wailing like most women would,
When he, to her the fairest of the nation,
    Her girlish choice, and that of womanhood,

A Tale of the Sea.

Was on the wild sea, and assailed by dangers,
    Struggling for life and love? Hap all was o'er!
These fearful thoughts were unto her no strangers,
    As filled with grief she wandered by the shore.

She was a lovely being; in each feature
    Innocence and love together smiled.
Nature alone made her so fair a creature,
    Artless simplicity's divinest child.
Eyes like the sky, whose language so beguiling
    Made the rapt lover deem her more than human,
Yet when her dimpled cheeks with joy were smiling,
    What could she be, if not a beauteous woman?

Her flaxen hair woven in dainty tresses
    Her soul-full eyes, her rose-on-lily cheek,
Expansive brow, which thoughtful mind expresses,
    Sweet mouth, rich lips, and nose of ancient Greek.
Pity and love were in each feature blended;
    A form proportionate, a temper mild;
'n her was nought her Maker could have mended,
    An angel-form bestowed on earthly child.

Thus earth she walked a spirit-incarnation,
    A God-soul dwelling in a human form,

The fairest damsel of the fair creation,
    Clad in flesh beauty, yet, like meanest worm
Subject to decay. Beauty like life is fleeting,
    Buds in our childhood, blossoms in our youth,
Ripens in manhood, and when age is seating
    Himself on wrinkled brows—'tis gone in sooth.

She was an orphan girl; for her dear mother
    Had long been dead, leaving her child alone
In a strange land homeless, until another
    Opened her heart-door, reared her as her own.
Old Widow Simmons with these children only,
    Lived in her cottage, pious, cheerful, poor ;
And no one feared, although it stood so lonely
    Under the cliffs, so near the ocean's roar.

Happy, and light, and cheerful as the morning,
    Over the dew-clad fields they both would pass,
Ere the sun rose the purple clouds adorning,
    Or their vast shadows flitted o'er the grass.
While fragrant perfumes through the air were winging,
    And waking flowers unfolding one by one,
While merry birds were in green hedgerows singing,
    The orphan maid strayed with the widow's son.

A Tale of the Sea.

Oh, passing sweet were their dear childhood rambles,
    Th' electric chain of feeling bound them fast,
Uniting them in all their happy gambols;
    In sunshine both, or else by clouds o'er cast;
And when life's early spring had passed them over,
    Within each bosom glowed love's vivid flame,
And sister, brother, were exchanged for lover,—
    Which, to their thinking, was a prettier name.

Oh, dear and happy time! when feeling's gushing
    From the deep fountain of the human heart,
When love's fire-thoughts are wildly o'er us rushing
    Like spring-tide floods; when the ideas start
From the brain-soil like the belovèd flowers
    Of tulip-spangled May; when life's dawn breaks
Into a morn of sunshine and of showers;
    When boyhood dies, and manhood first awakes!

When the life-force through arteries tingles,
    And soul reanimates this mass of clay;
When part with part and mind with mind commingles,
    And birds sing hymns of love on leafy spray;
When the rapt lover in the sea of feeling
    Doth madly plunge, fearless of pain or care,

Blind, senseless, deaf, intoxicated, reeling,
    Thus was it now with this love-stricken pair.

So years flew by—love's budding reached perfection,
    And he, true-hearted, wished to be made one ;
But Polly, provident, with more reflection,
    Said, " Put it off till Spring ; " and it was done.
O happy love ! thou pure, angelic passion,
    Based upon friendship, what a bliss art thou !
But, what a curse when yoked to tyrant fashion,
    That great law-breaker of the marriage vow!

The storm had ceased, yet, by the foaming water,
    Sweet Polly journeyed on intent with thought,
Until a soft voice said, " My lovely daughter,
    Oh, pray return, and rest within our cot."
" Oh, can I lay me down upon my pillow,
    And sleep, dear mother, till the morn, when he
Pale, drenched, and cold, is tossed upon the billow,
    Or hap, what's worse, asleep beneath the sea."

" Come, come, my daughter, cease to talk so wildly,
    For righteous Providence will prove his friend,"
Replied the dame in soothing accents mildly,
    As to the cottage they their steps did bend.

A Tale of the Sea.

"Retire to rest, my own belovèd Polly;
   It makes my old heart grieve to see thy tears.
To sorrow thus, my dearest child, is folly;
   'Tis heaping fuel on thy mouldering fears."

They reached the cottage, and the night passed sadly:
   But when fair morn arose within the sky,
She left her tear-bed, while her heart beat gladly,
   As forth she went, expecting him to spy.
She gazed, and as she gazed, what wild emotion,
   Anguish, and dread within her heart did swell,
For nought was seen upon the slumbering ocean;
   All, all was vacant,—down she senseless fell.

The good dame raised her, saying, "Almighty Power!
   Snatch not from me at once each lovely child!
Look down with pity! Oh, restore this flower!"
   She oped her eyes, and cried in accents wild,
"Oh, yes, he's gone, and I must soon be going!"
   "And wilt thou leave me then, my child, behind."
She gazed upon the dame, whose tears were flowing,—
   "Not with my own free will; for thou art kind!"

Day succeeded day, and yet the morrow
   Returned him not for whom they both did mourn.

Poor Polly lay upon her bed till sorrow
    Health's rosy hue from lily cheek had torn.
"My heart did tremble, when I from him parted,
    And sad forebodings rose within my breast.
Oh! shall I see him never! broken-hearted
    Must I live on till sweet death gives me rest."

Thus would she grieve, and by the ocean wander,—
    For many deemed her from that night insane,—
She'd sit upon the beach, on bye-gones ponder,
    Till time had worn away the greater pain.
Thus passed three years, and when the fourth was stealing, .
    Garland with spring flowers, o'er her lily brow,
Her heart rebounded with excess of feeling,
    To hear the birds sing from each leafy bough.

What pleasures do we feel when Spring is coming
    In all her beauty! when celestial dew
Falls on the flowers, and the melodious humming
    Of insects hail her! Need my muse tell you
That the immortal soul is then the dwelling
    Of thought too mighty to invest with words?
In rapture list! and when thy brain is swelling,
    Read all I think in the sweet songs of birds!

The rush of foaming waters o'er rocks bounding,
   The wind-song quivering through the young green leaves,
The lark-lay from above the rain-cloud sounding,
   And nature's varied tones that poet weaves
Into a spirit-hymn, the soul of beauty,
   And sends it over earth on lightning wings,
Missioned to teach man love and his God-duty,
   The child of his own mind and lovely spring.

Polly was good, and to her mother dutiful.
   Together would they wander in the vale
Viewing the works of God, sublime and beautiful,
   At eve and morn, when the refreshing gale
Filled air with incense. By a sparkling fountain
   God's holy book the good old dame would read,
Then with light hearts ascend a furze-clad mountain,
   And watch from its high crest the vessel's speed.

The grief of mind and anguish are past telling
   Which they then felt, for memory is cruel,
Making the poor heart grieve when with joy dwelling,
   As on love's fire it heapeth fancy's fuel.
Thus does it once more rouse the maid's distresses,
   Till pearly tears adown her pale cheeks run;

The dame is grieved, and with a thought-prayer blesses
    Departed husband, and her long lost son.

Can keen-eyed science, into nature peeping,
    Unfold the mystery of a sorrow-tear,
That from its fount of light comes gently creeping,
    Pure and transparent as its mother-sphere?
Can it unfold the blush of lovely maiden?
    Or how the spirit speaks through nerves from brain?
Or how, or why we're sometimes sorrow-laden,
    In bliss with gladness, or in woe with pain?

The source of life and light? of heat and motion?
    And the great force that makes and mars all things?
How the invisible gases form the ocean,
    The earth, stars, air, and gorgeous Saturn's rings?
What's life and thought? the soul immortal?
    And how, and when it enters into clay?
What the next world, and where, through whose dark portal
    All life must pass to everlasting day?

Alas! our little knowledge here is bounded;
    We know but little of the mighty plan

By which, from day to day we are surrounded,
   Or the life-soul that animates the man.
All is a mystery; life is but dreaming.
   We know not what we are, or what may be.
Nor shall, until the soul, like morning beaming,
   Rises in glory above this life's sea!

PART II.

Within a lovely meadow, where the daisy
   Gazed like a sainted spirit on the sky,
A shepherd boy lay stretched in day-doze lazy,
   While babbling brooklets sang his lullaby.
His soul was revelling in the land of fairy,
   Of tree, and flower, and gentle purling stream,
Of wingèd shapes in vision-thoughts so airy,
   That haunt the life-sphere of a poet's dream.

His was a lowly, yet a happy station,
   A kind of linnet-life on swinging spray,
Warbling thankofferings to the God-creation
   That rich in wondrous beauty round him lay.
Earth, air, and sea to him imparted gladness,
   The melodies of birds inspired his soul.

When rain-clouds veiled the earth in gloom and sadness
    He drooped as rose-bud 'neath their dark control.

In his mind-sphere the thought-world was unfolding
    Beauty divine, a fancy-painted scene,
Where the life-soul the plastic clay was moulding
    Into the loveliest forms that e'er were seen.
The splendours of the natural world were sinking
    Down in the mirrored heaven of his mind,
Where Fancy, the life-spirit wandered, thinking
    Mid rich-hued flower-buds trembling on the wind.

O God, and could Thy wisdom-spirit holy
    Dwell in the mind-dome of a shepherd boy,
Who dwelt in rustic cot with melancholy,
    Or skipped the hills with laughter-loving joy?
It was the time when sunny June was weaving
    For her dear Earth a beauteous chaplet gay,
When amorous Spring his blooming bride was leaving,
    And Summer breathing on the new-mown hay.

Voice-roused from sleep, the waking lad up-started.
    "Tell me, my boy, where 'Sea-rock Cottage' stands

A Tale of the Sea.

I will, sir, when these sleep-adhering lids have parted,
   And let the day-light in. Behold yon sands,
In which the billows break, where steep cliffs hoary
   Rush up to kiss the sky; turn thou that way;
For 'neath that shadowing, bold promontory
   Dwell two, with eyes as moist as salt-sea spray.

And when the busy earth is tired and sleeping,
   And tongueless silence holds her solemn reign,
In the sea-beach those sorrow-forms are weeping,
   With prayer-clasped hands in agonizing pain.
It is a mystery how they, broken-hearted,
   Can fondly cling to life by one small thread,
Can conjure up the scenes when they last parted
   From joy and hope, both sleeping with the dead.

But as the eye can view finite creation
   At one bright glance, and stamp it on the mind,
So memory, aided by imagination,
   Recalls sweet days time's flight has left behind.
Go to yon cottage, which tear-shedding Sorrow,
   Ghost-like, inhabits with her sister, Grief,
Where Hope keeps picturing a happy morrow,
   Bringing Despair instead of sweet relief."

"Before we part," in grief replied the stranger,
   "Oh, tell me, if thou canst, their sorrow's cause?
May heaven have saved my wife and child from danger;
   If not, I bow, my God, to thy just laws!"
"Twelve years ago, ah! well do I remember,"
   Began the lad; "though I was but a child,
Upon a cloudy day in drear November,
   The spirit o' storm lashed up the ocean wild.

"'Twas night,—and from the thunder-cloud was flashing
   The vivid lightning,—down poured rain and hail.
Foam-crested billows on the strand were dashing
   With roar terrific,—a light! a gun! a sail!
By the fire-flash, shrouded in foam and water,
   A ship was seen, hanging 'twixt sea and sky.
Above the wind, a voice was heard—'My daughter;
   Oh, save my child! Oh, hear a mother's cry!'

"The life-boat's manned, and o'er the billows sailing;
   Oh! Heaven preserve her in that awful sea.
Stout hearts scorn danger, and o'er death prevailing,
   Reach the wrecked vessel on the starboard lea.
But all in vain! for the surf-boiling water
   Dashes them back, leaving a gulf between.

A Tale of the Sea.

Lashed to the mast are mother and her daughter;
    The saddest sight that e'er these eyes have seen.

" With deaf'ning roar the wild waves are retreating
    Back from the beach, and o'er the vessel fly;
With thunder-crash, life-boat and ship are meeting.
    ' Hold fast! they're saved!' re-echo to the sky.
Another flash a horrid sight's revealing,
    The gasping ship a-struggling with a wave;
Darkness, and foam, and death are o'er her stealing,
    Down, down, 'mid shrieks, she sinks into her grave.

" 'Where is the life-boat?' every voice was crying,
    When the divided waters met once more.
See, by the torchlight, the little sea-skiff flying,
    Swift as the storm-wind, on towards the shore.
Bravely she skims along, o'er billows skipping;
    Guided by one inured to ocean-life.
' Throw out the grappling hook!' for she is dipping
    Into the wave-foam,—meeting the death-strife.

" Oh, God! they've missed! and amid shriek and wailing,
    In the sea's trough, on her beam-end she lies;
On comes the next wave, death upon it sailing,
    Spitting its fury madly in the skies.

Shoreward it rushes, mid the wild wind's yelling,
　King-wave o' the storm, awful to behold,
Seething, and surging, maelstrom-like, and swelling,
　Lashing the storm-cloud, till the blood runs cold.

"Like avalanche it comes,—is o'er them sweeping,
　Dashing the boat keel upwards on the strand,—
Like statues stand the crowd, trembling and weeping,
　To see a lady clasp with lily hand
A beauteous child; while with the other clinging
　In death's convulsions to a swimming man,
Who, like a seamew, o'er the waves is winging.
　Oh rush to aid them! save them if you can!

" And now, when wind and wave are shoreward flying,
　A rope is swiftly thrown within their reach.
Convulsively 'tis clutched by him a-dying,
　Who, the next moment's tossed upon the beach.
Pale as stem-broken lilies on the water,
　After a south-west blast has passed them o'er,
Thus lay entwined poor mother and dear daughter,
　With their preserver, on the shingle-shore.

"Sweat-drops of death were stealing down each feature,
　And the clock-ticking, ruckling sound was heard

Within the throat of that pale, dying creature,
　　Who strove to speak, yet could not lisp a word.
Fondly she clasped her child—the big tears starting,—
　　Her speaking eyes revealed her trust in God !
One struggle more !—hush ! the soul is parting
　　From that death-quivering—now, lifeless clod.

" O Death ! the terminus of life's history !
　　Thou fleshless, boneless, immaterial thing !
To the old world thou wert a mystery,
　　Until Lord Jesus did pluck out thy sting.
An angel-guide art thou from sphere terrestrial,
　　To flesh-imprisoned and pain-suffering soul ;
Opening the portals of a home celestial,
　　Where mutable earth-laws have no control.

" The storm ceased—morning dawned, and sun shone brightly ;
　　But what a ghastly scene did they display !
Bodies stiff and stark, which yestermorn were sprightly,
　　In death's embraces on the shingle lay !
Lifeless were many on that Sabbath morning,
　　When church bells called us to the house of prayer,
They heard no more that dulcet heavenly warning ;
　　The priest looked round,—their seats were vacant there !

"The voice of one in the loud anthem swelling
    Is silent now, that once made music sweet;
The honoured clerk, long on the amen dwelling;
    The child's preserver, empty was his seat.
He for full thirty years had braved the ocean,
    And many a life had saved from watery grave;
Yet now death struck him 'mid the storm's commotion
    In saving others.   Peace be with the brave!

"Within the churchyard, where nor yews nor willows
    Wave o'er their heads, their bodies are at rest;
No longer buffeted by life's rough billows,
    Their peaceful spirits are with angels blest.
The clerk's poor widow takes the sea-waif stranger—
    The beauteous orphan-girl—and makes her own.
Beneath her humble roof she shields from danger,
    With her own son, that dear one left alone.

" Time swiftly flew; and they did love each other.
    Like ivy clinging to its parent tree,
So did they fondly cling to their good mother.
    The boy a fisher was, and ploughed the sea.
Three years ago, one evening he departed,
    Leaving sweet Polly weeping on the shore.

A storm arose ; and she, most broken-hearted,
   Since that sad time of him heard never more.

" Farewell ! for now my sorrow-tale is ended.
   But one, alas ! of many that I know,
Learned by experience since these sheep I've tended,
   'Ere Beachy's warning light began to glow."
" Depart not yet,—this heart is almost broken !
   That shipwrecked vessel's name ?"   " *The Isabel*,
From India bound."   No sooner was this spoken,
   Than loud the stranger shrieked and senseless fell.

Down from the hill the orphan-maid came flying,—
   For she, at distance, heard that harrowing scream,—
Bathed his cold temples as he there lay sighing
   On a thyme-blooming bank by rippling stream.
His glazèd eyes unclosed their silken lashes
   As sorrow's tear-drops streamed adown his cheek.
What lovely vision on his eyesight flashes,—
   Fair as a sprite, as dew-eyed Pity meek ?

Swiftly he rose, and in his arms he caught her.
   " Am I in heaven ?   It is,—it is my child !
Peace to thy soul, dear wife !   O God ! my daughter !
   Thou beauteous image of thy mother mild !

As fondly round my neck thy arms are clinging,
    What dear associations upward rise !
Past times are o'er my memory-sphere now winging
    Swift as yon skylark soaring up the skies.

"Show me thy mother's grave, where she is sleeping
    Free from life's cares, beneath the green-grass sod;
Where I may pour my sorrow out in weeping,
    And ask sweet consolation of my God."
"Art thou my father? Am I awake or dreaming?—
    My mind was shipwrecked when my lover died.
Oh! is joy's sun on sorrow's world now beaming?
    And shall I smile again? Thank God!" she cried.

With tearful eyes, unto the churchyard slowly
    They bent their way; and, by a flower-clad grave,
Marked by a tombstone, with inscription holy,
    He sadly read: "Here lies Mary Palgrave,
Shipwrecked and drowned the thirteenth of November,
    One thousand seven hundred and ninety-seven.
Reader! shed tears for her sad fate. Remember
    That life is short. Prepare thy soul for heaven."

Down on the tender grass, with hands uplifted,
    With head and eyes raised skyward, down he fell;

And from a mind, with pure religion gifted,
    Poured forth a pious prayer, a God-sent spell,
Soothing the surges of a sea of trouble
    Into a perfect calm ; for He whose breath
Disperses navies like a water-bubble,
    Can heal a heart bruised by the hand of death.

There, as the grave-flowers—roses, pansies, daisies—
    Exhale their fragrance, which the winds waft high,
So God his pious soul-thoughts upward raises,
    And sends him in return a heavenly sigh,
Which fell upon him like the summer showers
    When earth is sun-scorched, and the grass seems dead,
Making it green again with buds and flowers,
    Though spirit, life, and beauty all had fled.

Night, with her gorgeous mantle, walked around him,
    Spangled with stars set in a field of blue ;
Yet there he knelt, for spirit-spell had bound him
    To the last home of her he loved so true.
The busy hum of day had all departed,
    Except the melody of one lone bird.
The grief-struck man exclaimed, as up he started,—
    "O God, I thank Thee that my prayer is heard !

"Come, my dear child, and lead me to thy dwelling,—
　To Sea Rock Cottage,—whither I was bound
When this death-tale burst o'er me, like the swelling
　Of ocean-floods, and struck me to the ground.
That was the port to which my bark was steering
　To learn its future course; where sweet relief
Should, like the sun 'bove sorrow-clouds appearing,
　Light up my mind-sky and dispel my grief.

"That awful morn, when waves the ship did smother,
　At the noon-hour elenge, depressed, and drear,
I saw before me stand your dear loved mother,—
　Pale as a lily, and I shook with fear.
She gazed upon me with a look of sadness;
　I rushed towards her,—there I stood alone;
Nothing was with me then but grief and madness;
　My blood grew chill, I seemed transformed to stone.

"Was it a dream, or real? Can man discover
　Whether departing souls can warn us here?
Or, if their disembodied spirits hover
　O'er those they love when quitting this life-sphere?
Oh! there are many mighty mysteries hidden
　From souls incarnate while upon this earth,

Momentous truths, which God has yet forbidden
   To be revealed until our second birth."

Their forms and voices in the distance faded
   Like waning echoes when the air is still.
Throughout infinity bright worlds paraded—
   Dwellings of souls which air, earth, ocean fill
With forms of beauty. Wind-lips were trembling
   Melodious sounds, as sweet as angels' song,
Breathing out fiery thoughts in notes resembling
   The eloquence divine of Nature's tongue.

O beautiful night! daylight's sleeping vision!
   Vivid reflection of celestial sphere!
That wisdom-orb, from whose bright clime elysian
   The souls of all things come! Spirit without fear
Bathes in thy life-sea, from exalted station,
   Free, disembodied from its mortal clod,
Surveys and comprehends the whole creation,
   And through all forms perceives the living God.

PART III.

PRELUDE.

BOYHOOD REMINISCENCES.

SWEET childhood scenes ! where, as a child, I wandered.
    Green and refreshing to my memory still
Is the rich valley where I often pondered,—
    The gurgling brook and wild-thyme blooming hill,—
The golden furze, on which the red-breast linnet
    Sang to his loved one setting on her nest,—
Old Harry's bush, with cuckoo calling in it,—
    Sea-cliff and mead are on my mind impressed.

There they are mirrored as the bright sun's shining,
    When clouds have vanished and the sky is clear,
And at all seasons, like green ivy twining
    Round some old tree whose autumn leaves are sere,
Cling to my soul. Ah ! sweetly o'er me creeping,
    Like blessèd sleep, is memory's music-strain ;
And in the past my present life is steeping,—
    I live in childhood days, and am a boy again !

The square-towered church, where many a pious pastor
    Had his flock guided on the heavenly road,—

The village school and its eccentric master,
    Fond of "grey weather," "shot-bag," "rope," and
    "rod."
Ah! woe betide the truant playing urchin,
    When blew his whistle at the hour of school,
Should he be absent; for his eye would search in
    Each vacant place,—black mark the lazy fool.

And the next morn, when he his pupils numbered,
    His eye would rest upon that truant's name,—
A death-like silence;' then his voice out thundered,
    "Sirrah, come hither!" and the trembler came.
Questions severe would follow, then confession
    With promises from duty ne'er to stray;
But "cat-o'-nine-tails" would make flesh-impression,—
    Nought else would satisfy stern William Way.

The school was William's kingdom, where in glory
    He sat upon his throne—three-legged stool,
From summer life-time until wintry hoary,
    Till hair grew grey, and blood began to cool.
He had a wondrous knack of story-telling,
    Of funny rhyming,—loved a jest and joke,

Besides the trick of sides with laughter swelling,
    And hiding his own mirth 'neath serious cloak.

But he is gone, and in the churchyard sleeping ;
    Dumb is the voice that once made urchins quake !
No more from out half-closèd lid is peeping
    That eye in sleep deemed shut, yet wide awake.
No more within Place House his voice is ringing,
    Another sways the rod,—is master there ;
Yet he will long be loved, for thought is springing
    From the brain-soil which he first tilled with care.

Leaf after leaf is memory unfolding,
    Like crimson petals of the opening rose ;
And I my shepherd-life am now beholding,
    Feeding my flock where crooked Cuckmere flows ;
Holding communion with the mighty spirit
    Which animates all life, and thinks in man ;
Love's richest legacy do I inherit
    In the dear scenes 'mid which my life began.

The town-elections,—music, din, and bustle ;
    The "running in" of each famed candidate ;
The feasting, drinking, hooting, and the tustle
    For seat in Parliament, and voice in State,—

A Tale of the Sea.

The lying, bribery, cheating, and slave-making.
　　The ruin and imprisonment for debt
In Dover Castle,—for like tigers slaking
　　Their thirst with blood, was e'er the winning set.

Oft by the cobbler's stall I'd stand and babble
　　Of politics and literature, ere I knew
Their A B C ; in poetry would dabble,—
　　The veriest rhymster of the rhyming crew.
But soon, 'mid clouds and sunshine, vale and mountain,
　　On thy rich grass, Wallsbrow, my mental sphere
Became illumined by that great light-fountain,
　　The world's poetic king,—her dear Shakspeare !

There oft with him my soul would hold communion,
　　Till earth was changed, the ocean and the sky ;
Between the three there seemed a spirit union,—
　　I looked on all things with a poet's eye.
Ah ! thou, of all men in this vast creation,
　　In mind approached the nearest unto God !
Great wisdom-teacher, spirit-incarnation !
　　Immortal heaven-soul animating clod !

In all my rambles over earth and ocean,
　　In my life-struggles.—and I've had my share,—

To thee my soul has turned with fond devotion,
    And thou hast soothed it when oppressed with care.
Farewell, great seer ! thy master-mind's opinion
    Now rules earth-dwellers with magician sway,
From pole to pole all bow to its dominion,
    Lord of all lesser lights ! bright star of day !

'Twas evening, and the winter sun was sinking
    Beneath the hills, and brightly gleamed the fire
Through the cot windows, as its guests were drinking
    Their social tea,—Dame, Polly, and her Sire.
And while the kettle on the hob was singing
    A merry stave, blended with crickets' song,
Old times revived, for memory back was bringing
    Life's youthful struggles that had slumbered long.

"Oh, I have deeply drunk of grief's potations,"
    Exclaimed the sire ; "the past seems but a dream.
This little cup, what dear associations
    Does it recall,—the trees, the murmuring streams,
Lawn, garden, flowers, and the manorial dwelling,
    My father sitting in his old oak chair,

A Tale of the Sea.

My mother, sobbing with the big tears swelling,
   The parting kiss!—oh, God! how fresh they are.

"To sea I went, and for nine years and over,
   My foot was planted not on English land;
In foreign climes I had been long a rover,
   And riches gained, when on this shingle strand
With tearful eyes, and heart all fondly beating,
   With hope's cup full, to see my friends once more,
My father with extended arms was meeting
   His long lost son, so loved in days of yore.

"But when about to sink in his embraces
   A press-gang seized me, and I fainted then.
'Twas vain contending that I was three paces
   In 'cinque port' bounds to these hard-hearted men;
Hurried away 'mid grief and execration
   From the good people and a father dear,
To serve, board man-of-war, my king and nation,
   With hopes frustrated, shedding many a tear.

"Twelve months from this, off India's sun-clime sailing
   With topsails reefed, under a stiff monsoon,
A pilot-boat with flag and gun was hailing
   Our gallant ship, which like cloud skimming-moon

Dashed through the billows ; quick her sails were fluttering
   In the wind,—with orders the boat upbore
For my release ; the captain, after muttering
   An oath or two, bade me be off ashore.

"When safe on land, I learned that application
   Was made to Parliament by this 'cinque-port,'
For my deliv'rance, which made me reparation
   With order signed and sent to me in short.
Thus was I freed by 'cinque-port town' protection,—
   By rights their vikings won in days of yore,—
Of which my seizure had been gross infraction,
   As they had pressed me 'bove the sea-washed shore.

"For a long time late in India did I tarry ;
   Increased in wealth, loved one, and sued her hard,
But was refused, and afterwards did marry
   Her sister, sleeping now in yon churchyard.
She soon presented me this sorrowing maiden,
   Like a young rose-bud steeped in morning dew ;
Our hearts with love and joy were overladen
   To see her mind bud as the body grew.

A Tale of the Sea. 47

"Time brought childhood, and in its wake came beauty,
    And on reflection we did both agree,
To train her properly t'would be our duty
    To send her to our home across the sea.
She sailed, accompanied by her dear mother,—
    You know the rest! I could not quit that coast
For many years; in the meantime, my brother
    Sent word they'd not arrived—mayhap were lost.

"To England come, I sought my father's dwelling,
    Wild weeds were flourishing where flowers grew.
I knocked, I hallooed, whilst my heart was swelling,
    And cold drops bathed my cheeks! I madly threw
The hall door open, and ran, loudly calling,
    Through the deserted rooms,—but found none there
To welcome me! Panes smashed and ceilings falling—
    Were cruel signs, alas! for my despair.

"With my poor brain on fire, behold me flying
    O'er leaf-strewn walk, and through the churchyard road,—
There father, mother, brother, all were lying,
    A tombstone told me,—gone to meet their God!

Down on the green grass graves I fell heart-broken,
    Life valueless to me, although the heir
Of rich domains, and the parental token,
    The family mansion, with its old oak chair!"

"Oh, can it be!—it is my dear young master!
    The cup thou hast was thine in happier days,"
Replied the dame, while the big tears flowed faster
    Adown each cheek. "How wondrous are Thy ways,
Almighty God! Art thou that cherub creature
    Which oft, as girl, I dandled on my knee?
Oh, what a change! so pale, so thin,—each feature
    Stamped with the seal of care and misery!

"Take heart! for sorrow cannot last for ever;
    Passions of man, like sea-tides, ebb and flow;
Death but a little while doth from us sever
    Our dearest friends, who unto glory go!
But we shall meet again, where grief and sadness,
    Darkness and change, and death have no control;
Burst through this life-cocoon to a world of gladness,
    A disembodied, free, immortal soul!"

Time spread his wings. Yet though of higher station,
    Polly would never leave that humble cot,

A Tale of the Sea.

Which at all seasons was her habitation,
    From whence she oft would wander to the spot,
That heard their last adieus in words love-telling,
    Sinking like music in sweet memory's cell,—
There, when the sea of thought was wildly swelling,
    She'd lull its storms by uttering that farewell.

The day was beautiful, the flowers were springing,
    And summer warblers sang divinest lays,
The village bells were changes sweetly ringing,
    And all earth echoed with responsive praise.
Upon the daisied turf she stood this morning,
    In a day-dream, whilst love-beguiling smiles
Illumed her features, like the sun adorning
    His beauteous bride, the gem of ocean isles.

She cast her blue eyes, rivalling heaven's brightness,
    On the calm sea, that slumbered like a child;
Espied a ship,—and boat which sped with lightness
    Over the blue expanse. With gestures wild
She hailed it; her sensitive heart with gladness
    Began to beat as it had oft before,
Till memory dawned, and "He is gone!" with sadness
    Ejaculated she, then left the shore.

She entered in her little cottage, weeping
    To think that Fancy still should lead astray
Her nobler reason, and Memory, o'er her creeping,
    Picture to her joys that long had flown away.
Pensive she sat while heart and brain were swelling,
    And the late smiles of happiness did mar,—
She heard a voice, "What cheer ho! in this dwelling?
    Wilt give a welcome to an honest tar?"

"That voice!" she cried. "Ye Powers that o'er me hover,
    It must be his! I know its sound too well."
"It is, sweet Polly! 'tis thy own true lover."
    She rushed towards him, in his arms she fell.
You oft have seen a lovely flower in blossom,
    When morning's pearls of dew weigh down its head,
Sink for support upon the earth's fair bosom,
    So Polly drooped as senseless as the dead.

"Cheer up, my Polly! Long time have I striven
    To meet thee with a firm, true-bearing heart.
Let this love-kiss thy beauteous cheeks enliven
    With smiles angelic." She from her swoon did start,
Gazed on her lover, fell upon his shoulder,
    Her bright eyes beaming through a flood of tears,

A Tale of the Sea.

"Oh, blissful rapture thus to behold her;
    True and more lovely after three long years!

"My mother! Do these arms once more enfold thee?
    Weep not, but let this day be one of joy."
"Thanks be to God that I once more behold thee,
    Joy of my widowhood, my dear, dear boy!"
"But who is this, my mother?" "I would rather
    Polly should answer that," replied the dame;
Who with a rose-blush said, "It is my father,
    Whom God had given me, before you came."

"But will he give me you?" 'Mid tears and blushes
    She gazed upon her sire, who slyly threw
At her a meaning glance, that made love's flushes
    Suffuse her cheeks as in his arms she flew.
"Like your own hearts your hands shall be united."
    Replied the sire. "But what have you to tell
Since the dread night when Polly was affrighted
    At the wild storm, when her you bade farewell?"

"Come, sit you down, and hear my simple story;
    How I escaped, through Providence, a grave.

The lightning flashed, the thunder rattled o'er me ;
    The wind arose ; the sea began to rave ;
Far from the land, storm-waves around me roaring ;
    Each rag of canvas soon was blown away.
Sometimes to heaven my little skiff was soaring,
    And then again engulphed in sea and spray.

"I need not paint to you the bitter anguish
    Nor the death-fears that round my vision flew.
Like dying babe, my boat began to languish,
    When in the east a ship appeared in view.
She walked the billows like a wingèd fairy,
    As swift as fancy in her mad career ;
The storm-waves were to her but bubbles airy,
    She tossed them gaily in the atmosphere.

"On, on she came, while vaulted dome did rattle
    With booming thunder crackling over head ;
A noble ship she was, full armed for battle,
    For her death-roaring cannons, foemen's dread,
Through the wild air their voices grand were sounding,
    In answer to the signal that I gave.
Her seamen snatched me from death's fears surrounding ;
    To lead a life of glory with the brave.

A Tale of the Sea.

"At length by courage did I gain promotion,
   And under Nelson did my rank maintain,
As true and stainless as a son of ocean,
   And glory fell upon me like the rain.
'Twas at Trafalgar for this Isle of Beauty
   Our great commander cried, 'England expects
That every man this day will do his duty;'
   And every gallant tar obeyed the text.

" The signal given by our isle-defender,
   Pell-mell we fell upon the gallant foe,
Broke through their lines, and forced them to surrender;
   Fear palled their courage, and they fled below.
Late where their colours on the winds were flying,
   Now flew our own, amid the huzza roar
Mingled with groans of wounded and the dying,—
   But, oh, our brave commander was no more!

"The moment that he heard we were victorious,
   He gave unto the winds his parting breath;
While Victory's warlike spirit hovered o'er us,
   He closed his eyes in the sweet sleep of death!

Long may his name sail down the stream of ages,
 And Nelson live within our realms afar;
For Fame's engrossed it in her glorious pages,
 The noblest patriot and the bravest tar!

"And may our England, in the time of danger,
 Lead on her sons, then 'nought will make them rue;'
She'll overcome in fight each saucy stranger,
 'If England to herself do rest but true!'
So now, dear Polly, in our cot together,
 Let's live and love from battle's fierce alarms;
We've braved the roughest of blind Fortune's weather,
 And now, becalmed, we'll anchor in her arms."

Thus angel Virtue, which these lovers guarded
 From sin's foul snares and folly's luring voice,
With bliss at length their faithfulness rewarded;
 Contentment made them smile and health rejoice.
Poor lovelorn maid! cast not a look disdainful
 On this Sea-Tale; but know, sweet girl, that this
Which at the present time is dark and painful,
 Is oft the messenger of future bliss.

My tale is ended ; every leaf turned over
   Until their comes a blank, like life's last breath :
For the bright world beyond a veil does cover,
   Floating this side the shadow-land of death.
Both good and evil in this world are blended,
   Where good from evil springs, evil from good :
And will until this changeful life is ended,
   And soul meets soul before its Maker—God !

RHODA MARTEN.

OBIIT SEPTEMBER 2ND, 1840.

THOU sleep'st, sweet Rhoda, now the sleep of death !
Those bright reflectors of the God-like mind
Are closed, like flowers uprooted by the breath
Of a rude storm ! Thy spirit, unconfined,
Free as a thought, soars lightly on the wind,
Cleaving the air with its ethereal wings,
Swift as a sunbeam to the starry spheres !
Thy body lies dead to the murmurings,
The sorrowing, and sighing of thy loved compeers !
Oh, God ! those beauteous cheeks, on which the rose
Did sweetly blossom, fed by pearly tears,
Are lily pale ! Though bright life's morn arose,
Giving sweet promise of a day more fair,
Yet clouds crept o'er, and all was darkness there !

A DAY-DREAM.

1841.

The sails were set; we ploughed the sea
  As swift as the wind-driven clouds;
The heaving billows began to roar;
  The wind whistled through the shrouds.

The day grew dark; the lightning curled
  Like snakes along the sky.
We hove her to, her sails we furled,
  And heaved a bitter sigh.

" A brighter day did never begin
  To streak the balmy air.
Oh, who would crawl o'er this world of sin,
  A desert of despair!

" Snatch me to better world, sweet Death,
  No beauty in this I see."
'Twas thus I cried as heaven grew dark,
  And the winds howled fearfully.

Then they sank to sleep, and calmly the sea
    In breathless silence lay;
When a spirit so fair appeared in the air,
    As white as the snowy spray.

That lovely Spirit hung o'er my head,
    Like a star in the rich blue sky;
Or the morning lark a fanning the air,
    And singing his lullaby.

Not a sound was heard in the silent air,
    Not a murmur rose from the sea,
As the voice of that Spirit sweetly sung
    Its heaven-born melody.

Song of the Spirit.

There's a spirit of beauty in earth that gleams
Like the sheen of the day-star's lustrous beams,
That makes her face lovely, and entrances
The poet's soul with her smiling love-glances.

A Day-Dream.

The flame-coloured insects are flitting along,
Like meteors o'er heaven, with musical song,
And the grasshopper's chirp is merry to hear,
Among the tall grass, as summer draws near.

On the breath of the gale the cornfields wave,
Like delicate reeds as they gracefully lave
In the rippling stream when the wind rushes by,
With its spiritual love-chanting melody.

The wild bee sippeth the sweets from each flower,
And the many-hued butterfly seeketh his bower,
As rich in his colours, as gorgeous and fair
As the rainbow, loveliest vision of air.

Walk 'neath the shade of the leaf-budding boughs,
Where the warblers of spring are plighting their vows,
In language as sweet as spirits can
Pour forth and enrapture the soul of man.

The souls, disembodied, of flowers take wing,
And float on the gale, whose murmuring
Is the echo of spirits' aërial songs,
And the wind is the breath that to them belongs.

The moon's silver rays that play on a stream
In the visions of night, when the planets gleam
Like pearls, reflecting the sun's gold hue,
Piercing the veil of night's lovely blue,

Revealing the vastness of heaven's steepness
In the clear water's awful deepness,
Are not so bright as the Earth shines there,
The loveliest world enveloped in air.

Beautiful Earth! if you did but know
How spirits delight to wander below,
'Twould make you love dearly what now you despise,
The gem of the worlds that circle the skies.

Those fertile spots, and those valleys green,
Those waving cornfields that intervene,
The cowslip meadows, the furze-clad hills,
The bright blue sea, and the rippling rills,

Are sights that oft make the spirit's eye
Dart love-streaming glances down through the sky;
Which some mistake for a shooting star,
Or the silver lightning of worlds afar.

A Day-Dream.

They are eye-rays of love that flit to the soul
Of life-cycling Earth as we over her roll.
When they rush through her air, as down they're driven
These soul-rays resemble the bright stars of heaven.

Earth's troubles and cares, which your feelings depress,
Dissolve in the sunshine of happiness:
Like the scud of the sea as a ship rushes by,
Flitting like life to eternity.

Yet you are miserable, and will be
As long as a wave is seen on the sea,
Or a cloud passes over the bright blue sky,
For such is your life's destiny!

The sweet day-dream of your youth is gone,
Which shone as bright as the spirit of dawn,
Spreading its loveliness here and there,
Crimsoning the face of the murky air.

Look back on the past, and what does it seem?
A bubble that floats for a while on a stream,—
A springtide of love and blossoming flowers,
That's vanished away 'mid sunshine and showers!

You waste the bright present, complaining of grief,
And hoping to-morrow may bring you relief,—
Peevish and restless keep journeying on—
Sip the sweetness of youth, when youth is gone.

The earth is a beautiful spot, I ween
That worlds above are not brighter seen ;
But man's evil passions predominate so
That he filleth the heart of his brother with woe.

Woe to earth's tyrants at that awful day
When spirits assemble in solemn array,
In God's mighty presence, arraigned for the deeds
Committed on earth ! Those foul passion-weeds

That long have o'errun the fair garden of truth,
Ploughing furrows of age on the smooth brow of youth,
Will then be uprooted and cast on the winds,
Till time shall have bleached their sin-spotted minds.

Time past was the same as the future will be,
For the changes of earth are like those of the sea :
The tempest rolls o'er it, like thoughts o'er the mind ;
'Tis gone ; not a trace of its fury behind !

A Day-Dream.

Time's billows have swept over nations of old,
Shipwrecked mighty empires, and low in the mould
Their ruins have buried; Death's poison-blast then
Swept away, as it now does, the children of men.

Then act in the present; dream not on the past,
Nor live in the future; for life is too vast
A theatre of action, of wisdom and worth,
To be frittered away by a child of the earth.

Life, Death, Eternity! dread not each name;
Though seeming to differ, yet still they're the same:
Bound up in man's soul, like rays of the sun,
They diverge for awhile, then mingle in one.

The soul never dies; merely changes its form
Through all its life-phases, the same as the worm,
Which crawls on the leaf, spins its coffin, and dies,
Then bursts its death-prison, and sports in the skies!

  The vision fled, and I paced the deck
   While the good ship on did fly,
  Scudding the billows, till not a speck
   Of the white cliffs met my eye.

And life's hope-star rose in my breast
   Dispersing my evil mood ;
And I turned to my duty with such a zest
   As a hungry man to his food.

———o———

AUTUMN.

THE life-spring fled and the summer came,
    And burnt leaf and grass with her fiery breath;
And tinged the corn with her golden flame,
And the harvest moon and the evening sky;—
    Preparing a path for old Winter—Death,
Who shortly must pass by!

Then the birds were still, and the nights grew chill,
    And the red leaves whirled around;
And the sweet flower-stalks did rot on the walks,
    And tortoises crept under ground.

And the skeleton trees chattered in the breeze,
    And the life-sap fled to the roots;
And the wild winds flew till they hurricanes blew,
    And tumbled the ripened fruits.

Then the stars from on high, through a clear blue sky,
    With smiles looked out on the night,
Till the clouds 'gan to lower, and a sheeted shower
    Made the old earth quake with affright;

For it tumbled down as if it would drown
    The country and town in its flight !
Till Autumn's rich dower of corn, fruit, and flower,
    That gladden the sight, and give us delight,
Were blasted by Winter's death-frown !

Who, with icy wand, next rode o'er the land
    On the wings of an arctic blast !
Uprooting and tearing, growling and scaring,
    Till naked and cold, teeth-chattering and old,
Poor Autumn, despairing,
    From his frost-lash shrank back aghast,
To hide herself under the ground.
    But the Tyrant seized on her delicate form ;
And tore it, and crushed it, and whirled it around ;
He ice-locked the earth veins, which, when he had done,
He pelted her sore with his snow-and-hail storm,
    And shut up the light of the sun !

———o———

THE DYING MAIDEN.

'Twas morn, and calm was earth and heaven;
Still was the day that God has given,—
The Sabbath-day, of days most blest,
That towers sublimely o'er the rest!
And not a wave of air was stirred
To drown the notes of one sweet bird,
Which sat and sang upon a stone,
As if the world were all his own.

Through vale and plain the rivulet
    Appears a silken, winding thread,
Glistening like a diamond, set
    In a crown on monarch's head,
Or a lily dew bewet!

Dancing, rippling, ever going
    Merrily o'er its shingle bed;
Let the world say what it may,
Still by that sweet cot 'tis flowing
    With its fairy-footed tread,
Where the sweetest flowers are blowing,
    To gem the coronet of Day,
    And deck his regal head!

The Dying Maiden.

Through the rose-embowered windows
    Stream the sunbeams on the floor;
Eglantine and sweet moss-roses,
    With honeysuckles climb the door,
    And gem with flowers the entrance o'er.
As if the Fays had gathered posies
To beautify that humble dwelling
    For now and evermore.

The sound of distant ocean rolling,
    Strikes upon the listening ear,
Mixed with village church bells tolling
    Sons of God to worship there!
Sweetly chime they soft and clear,
In music sweet as angel-voices
    Echoing in the stilly air!

In the cottage sleeps a maiden,
    Snowy-white her lily cheek,
And her eyes, with big tears laden,
Show the mind's awake in dreaming,
    And that sorrow-tears will leak
From their founts, in splendour beaming,
    Plainly to the gazers telling
    Grief-floods in her bosom swelling.

The Dying Maiden.

She breathes, she wakes, 'mid fearful sighing,
    While the watchers hold their breath ;
For the immortal soul is flying,
    And they tremble before Death !
Upon the coverlit is lying
    Her little dog, with human heart,
His large eyes gazing on her fondly,
    Seeming to say, we'll never part.

Lovingly he her hand caresses,
    And his bright expressive eye,
Speaks his thoughts, " You must not die ; "
Then buries his head beneath her tresses,
And heaves a human sadful sigh ;
    In grief was murmured many a blessing ;
And many a tear bedewed each eye,
    To witness feeling so distressing.

Oh, holy, pious, beauteous feeling !
    That purifies the inner man,
When sorrow-fits are o'er us stealing,
And the mind is staggering, reeling,
    And the cheeks are pale and wan !
Let us bear it, for its stings

The Dying Maiden.

Will teach the soul to leave her dwelling,
And in God's thought world try her wings!

As slowly fades the flickering taper,
   Fanned by every little breath,
Bursting into life the stronger
   The nearer it approaches death;
So flickers life in Eleanore,
   Only to burn a little longer,
   Like the bubbles on a river,
Swimming, sparkling, 'mid the roar
   Of ocean-tides, then fade for ever.

The gulf is passed, life's storm is over,
   Death hath done his worst! the soul,
   Endowed with immortality,
Flits to purer worlds above her,
   Sees unfold God's wisdom-scroll,
And reads His mighty mysteries
   Enshrined in letters brighter far
   Than golden sun-thoughts, or the star
That 'mid the hosts of heaven flies!

Tearful eyes are weeping sadly,
   Parent, friend, companion, lover;

The Dying Maiden.

Bowed by grief which sinks them madly
In the unfathomed sea of feeling,
  Nor will peace above them hover,
Till hope like golden morn comes stealing
  Above the surging waves of grief,
And with her heavenly spirit gladly
  Soothes their sorrows, gives relief!

—— o ——

A LOVE LETTER.

TO MISS BEAL.

JANUARY 1ST, 1845.

I GREET thee, lady, on this new-year morn
With a love letter, whose contents I fear
He o' the golden bow did not inspire,
But Bigot Credo, who condemns my soul
To everlasting torment with the fiends :
And deems the earth we tread upon a hell,
Which is a little paradise of bliss,
Where the embodied soul, in doing good,
Can bravely work out that regeneration,
Which fits it for a higher, purer life !
Our little world, lapt in its airy sphere,
Is but the shadow of the real, which lies
Around about it. The departed souls
Of those that lived to die, and died to live,
Are with us still, hid by th' electric veil
That shrouds their forms divine from human eyes.
Oh, yes ! they whisper comfort to our ears,
Cheering afflicted spirits pent in clay,

A Love Letter.

Subject to all the strange mutations,
Matter must undergo.

      The soul's the man,
And man alone ! eternal, infinite,
That vivifies the elements, and moulds
Them into a dwelling-place. The brain's the throne
On which the spirit sits, and governs all ;
The nerves electric wires, where thoughts do course
Up, down, around, about, man's microcosm ;
The heart, great fount of life, his ocean is,
The arteries rivers, veins the streams,
And pores the sluices of his continent.
Man is creation's masterpiece ; perfect
In every part, the apex of myriad shapes
That live and move ; and all the mighty laws
That govern matter, work in him alone !
Then is the latest, best divine creation,
This wondrous life-machine, the spirit's home,
A thing to be despised and loathed ? Oh, no !
Bigots, sectarians, narrow-minded men
Are so from imperfection—should not rule,
But must be ruled. Madmen and criminals
From unequal organization spring,

And should be treated kindly. The mind diseased
Needs careful moral training ;—then why hang
The murderer? whose abnormal brain's the cause
Of that great sin. Everywhere you'll find that
Imperfection sins, perfection worketh good !
Pity the sinner, then, but hate his crime,
And treat him as you would do the insane ;
For had his brain been perfect, so would he.
Bear with the atheist too, who sees no God
Through all the wondrous works that strike his eye,
For though he be in intellect a giant,
In morals he's an idiot !

      Despise not, then,
God's beauteous works, but love them, most of all
That masterpiece made in His image—man.
The earth's my temple, and the glorious sky,
Spangled with living orbs, its vaulted roof.
To me the smallest leaf, the meanest thing
That crawls upon it, the dust we tread on,
And the minutest drops of silver dew,
Kissing the ruby lips of budding rose,
The tiny insect living on its leaves,
Or the still smaller one on which it feeds,—

A Love Letter.

Life within life, mystery in mystery,—
Are wisdom-lessons Nature sets for man.
All these effects of some great ruling·cause,
Lift up my soul unto the Cause of all,
And dimly through the veil of His omnipotence
I see my Maker—God!

LINES

ON THE OPENING OF THE BRIGHTON WORKING MAN'S INSTITUTE.

OCTOBER 23RD, 1848.

INSCRIBED TO ITS PRESIDENT,
SIR JOHN CORDY BURROWS KNIGHT.

Up, up ! and let us be doing ;
   For mind we must brighten, not rust !
Up, up ! and let us soar higher,
   Not wallow like swine in the dust.

It is a bright world where the eagle
   Soars up like a flame to the sky ;
Sees the green world rolling beneath him
   With his cloud-piercing, telescope eye.

Shall the image of God be earth-crawling,
   While a bird in the sky soareth higher ?
O man, unprison thy spirit,
   And bid it to heaven aspire.

Work, work ! and never be idle,—
   Think not of this world as your home;
But bring out of dust the pure spirit,
   For its home's in a world to come.

Teach, teach ! the most ignorant nation
   Is eager to learn all it can ;
And 'tis a wise law of creation,
   That man must regenerate man !

Seek wisdom in depths of the ocean—
   In the air-wingèd world, sea, and land,
Keep body and mind e'er in motion,
   And God's divine laws understand.

Preach the progress march intellectual
   From the pulpit, ye priest of the church ;
Lest the laity cease to respect you,
   And leave you behind in the lurch.

On, on ! never cease to be going,
   But progress while God gives you breath ;
Then up ! and let us be doing,
   And work the good work until death !

SPRING TIME.

1850.

In spring I walk in meadows,
  Inhale the breath of health,
While music wakes around me,
  And Nature shows her wealth.
The rainbow-coloured flowers,
  The winds that o'er them pass,
The life-awakening showers
  That warble on the grass,

The green boughs gently waving
  To brooks that gurgle by,
Within whose crystal waters
  Are imaged earth and sky,
The nightingale's rich warble,
  The whitethroat's lively trill,
The throstle's merry whistle,
  From copse beneath the hill,

The sky with all its wonders,
  The water-bearing cloud,
The lightning-flash so brilliant,
  The thunder-peal so loud,

Spring Time.

Each little clod and mountain
    Was made from one God-plan :
Earth, air, sea, lake, and fountain,
    Birds, fishes, beasts, and man.

All forms that lie around us
    Display His wisdom-power,
From dewdrop to the twinkling star,
    From pollen to the flower.
There is a mind enfolded
    In every living thing,
By which its form is moulded
    And beautified in spring.

As tidal-waves of ocean
    Flow on from pole to pole,
So mind is set in motion,
    And animates the whole.
These life-rays of creation
    All centre into one,—
Mysterious, bright, and beautiful,
    As in yon living sun.

Eye hath not seen His glory,
    But spirit feels His power,

Spring Time.

Quivering 'neath His finger-touch
    As does the sweet wind-flower.
His soul-rays dart within us,
    We live upon His breath,
Then die, to rise in glory,
    Like spring from winter-death!

SOUL EMBODIMENTS.

1851.

CALM is this April day; the air is sweet!
And earth hath mighty heavings 'neath our feet;
The trembling spirits strive to burst the tomb
Where Winter chained them in perpetual gloom.
A fairy soul from heaven wings her way,
Arrayed in sunbeams lovelier than the day;
She passes o'er the meadows, clad in green,
While the life-sun through purple clouds is seen
Beaming with smiles upon his bride, the Earth,
Who from her snowy mantle issues forth;
Above her head the soaring skylarks sing,
Beneath her feet the blossomings of spring
Receive her footfall. Budding trees and flowers
Salute her gracefully! swift-footed showers
Before her dance, humming their mystic song,
As over blades and leaves they skim along.
How the air trembles! Nature holds her breath!
Listening like child to what that spirit saith:
" Ye trees, put forth green buds; ye flowers, blow

Sweet warblers, sing; and rippling waters, flow;
Ye wingèd fays, now flit o'er all this scene,
Sprinkle your sun-force, clothe the land in green,
Steep in the rainbow-hues the flowers and skies,
Till earth appears a new-born paradise!"

The unchained spirits wander o'er the earth,
Which, at their touch, conceives, and life has birth;
Before the mystery-veil, Dame Nature's pall,
The life-forms rush, with wonder strike us all.
Hark! how the rich and myriad-voicèd song
In floods of rapturous music rolls along!
Trembling awhile on leaves it bounds and jars,
Then floats in volumes up among the stars:
Earth's great thank-offering to its God above,
Who, in return, sends sunshine, light, and love.

Why seeks the mortal eye to look behind
Life's holy veil, and see the world's great mind
Embodying souls in different forms of clay,
To work His great designs, then pass away?
To see if spirits take life-forms again,
And, walled in flesh, endure its ills and pain;
Or, purified, depart to brighter spheres,
For ever freed from this sad world of tears!

Soul Embodiments.

Why should we wish God's secrets to explore,
Life's gordian knot untie—to heaven soar?
Has the soul wisdom of these hidden things,
While in her prison-house she folds her wings,
Wishing in airy regions far to sail
Beyond the ken, behind the secret veil?
Oh! mystery of mysteries! God's life-plan,
He never did, nor will, reveal to man;
We must be born, and live, and walk in gloom,
To look behind the veil, pass through the tomb!

TO ARTHUR SIENKIEWICZ, ESQ.

1859.

POLAND, the brave, trod down by victors oft;
    Enchained by vulcan tyrants to her soil,
Soon may her white-plumed eagle soar aloft,
    And give blest freedom to her sons of toil!

May hope arouse the exile's joy once more,—
    Poland arise, and her brave children then
Shine forth as bright as in the days of yore,
    And chase the northern bear into his den.

Though "Freedom shrieked as Kosciusko fell,"
    She did not die, but will arise again;
And from her sky-throne hear the dying yell
    Of her stern tyrant stretched upon the plain.

When the wild Turk knocked at Vienna's gate,
    When Austria motionless before him lay,
Great Sobieski snatched her from her fate,
    And made the turbaned bigot kiss the clay.

To Arthur Sienkiewicz, Esq.

Europe was saved by Polish sword and lance,
   And hymns and acclamations pealed aloud
Through Germany, and Holland, England, France;
   And nations loved her, and before her bowed.

Yet, when oppressed by that ungrateful host
   Which she had saved from Moslem rites and sway,
The English sentinel slept at his post,
   And Gallic warrior deafly turned away.

Then the white eagle, by her friends forsaken,
   Was pounced on by a flock of vultures base;
That carrion flock, from off whose backs she'd shaken
   Those birds less vile of Asiatic race.

Where were the chivalry and swords of France?
   Where were the dauntless troops of England then?
Oh, not one British sword or Gallic lance
   Flashed forth to save this noble race of men!

Alone they left them, vainly to contend,
   To fight for freedom, tyranny to brave;
To strugggle onward without hope or friend,
   To leave their country or become a slave.

The mark of infamy is on each brow,
    The brand of shame is burning on each heart.
Not from her eyry did the eagle bow !
    Not from his lair did sleeping lion start !

Cheer thee, poor exile, wandering forth alone ;
    The tyrant's kingdom's based upon the sand !
Freedom's avenging God is on His throne—
    Waves, fire, and thunder issue from His hand !

The heavens tremble—vivid lightnings fly ;
    The ocean rages—wind 'gainst wind is hurled ;
The wings of darkness cover all the sky ;
    The nations fear, and earthquakes rend the world !

But Freedom's spirit soars above the strife,
    Like Mercy's angel when the fight is done !
From evil, good springs forth; from death, new life ;
    When clouds dissolve, more brightly shines the sun !

'Neath Poland's ashes smouldered freedom's light,
    When the poor exile left his parent-sod ;
The western nations hailed him with delight,
    And freedom's cause became the cause of God !

Poets arose, and with a flaming pen
  Scorched their deep sufferings in the book of fame ;
The world gave birth to angels like to men,
  Crowning with glory Dudley Stuart's name !

The Polish exile was his son and heir—
  He clothed and loved him, all his wants supplied ;
Consoled and cheered him with a father's care ;
  Fought all his battles—in his just cause died !

And when o'er his loved body closed the earth,
  The grateful Poles to heaven their prayers did raise,
And stamped a medal to his matchless worth :
  Let nations give to both their meed of praise.

Spring will awaken o'er the Polish land,
  And, like a flood-tide, happiness shall spread !
While Freedom's spirit, 'neath the Almighty's hand,
  Shall rise, like Lazarus, from the sleeping dead !

When in your own sweet home, dear Sienkiewicz,
  When Poland free shall choose her own free king,
When you're surrounded by the gay and rich,—
  Oh, think of him whom you inspired to sing !

To Arthur Sienkiewicz, Esq.

The songs of France upon our British shore,
    When first you lisped our Anglo-Saxon tongue,
Picking up gold-thoughts from that precious store,
    Which our great poets o'er the land have flung!

Farewell! God's blessings on thee and thy race!
    May earthly comforts unto thee be given;
And should we here no more meet face to face,
    Then let us hope, through Christ, to meet in heaven!

SONNETS COMPOSED IN 1859.

ON THE REV. F. W. ROBERTSON, M.A.

I.

THOU wert a fire-tongued messenger of heaven,
A man of noble brow and loving heart,
To whom a dower of high-souled truth was given
In eloquence divine ! Nor guile, nor art,
Nor bigotry accursed flowed from thy tongue ;
But rills of genius from truth's fountain came.
Breathless and rapt the congregations hung
Upon the heaven-born music of thy speech,
Which rent the rich man's heart like wingèd flame,
And purified his soul. And thou didst teach
The humble sons of toil, thy "BROTHER MEN,"
To fight life's battle as they onward trod.
Earth's tyrants quailed beneath thine eye and pen,
But good men honoured thee, TRUE PRIEST OF GOD !

II.

His soul was full of poetry that gushes
Up from deep feeling's well, a purling stream !

With voice of music, like the bird that hushes
A witching night of June ; when the moonbeam
Silvers th' enamelled leaves of forest trees.
He was a man of perfect heart divine ;
A soul embodiment that once did shine
Near the eternal throne ; and by degrees
Did raise his brother-man to that bright sphere
In which he dwelt before God sent him here !
Of pre-existence I have shadows dim ;
It is my creed that souls can never die ;
That we in other worlds have lived like him ;
That we again shall meet him in the sky !

ENGLAND.

I.

THOU Island-Queen, kissed by the loving sea,
Whose silver foam-wreath laves thy hallowed sod,
Home of great minds, altar of freedom's God,
Earth's sacred fane, inviolate and free !
Throned on the rocks for ages hast thou stood,
Braving the wild waves, thunder, wind, and flame ;

Shedding for freedom's cause thy richest blood,
While nations, awe-struck, bowed before thy name.
Through the dim cloud-veil raise thy awful brow,
And from thy sea-throne gaze upon the shore,
Where envious meanness at thy greatness now
Chafes, plots, and scowls as in the days of yore.
Awake, great spirit ! shake thy wings and cry,—
" Fight for your island-home—be free or die !"

II.

Lovely is England, with her green hedgerows :
Her cottages and gardens filled with flowers,
Sweet shady nooks where gipsies pass their hours,
Where sings the nightingale and streamlet flows.
Land of the violet and the sweet moss rose,
Daisies and golden furze, and leafy bowers,
Where sunshine mingles with refreshing showers.
Birthplace of freedom, feared by all her foes,
Whose universal tongue and flag unfurled
Carry her blessings over all the world !
Oh, how I love her and the ocean waters
That lave her shores, her green lanes, hills, and dells,
The voices of her lovely sons and daughters,
And the rich music of her merry bells.

BEACHY HEAD.

THY giant form, bold headland, cleaves the sky;
A bulwark 'gainst the ocean's rage art thou!
Time on his whirlwind pinions hath swept by,
And nations buried, since thy awful brow
First frowned upon the flood as it frowns now;
Laughed it to scorn and echoed back its cry,
Ere Roman warrior trod thy summit high,
Or the Phœnician mariner did plough
These pathless seas! when with a mighty motion
Thou and thy brother hills first leaped from ocean!
As thou for countless ages hast withstood
Th' invading ocean rushing on thy strand,
So may we stand and shed our dearest blood,
To guard from foreign foe our native land!

BRIGHTON.

SKY-CROWNED, in regal beauty on twin hills,
Parted by winding vale of foliage green,
Fair Brighton stands, of watering places queen!
The fame of whose inspiring breezes fills

The world with wonder. How gorgeously,
A league of palaces ! she skirts the sea,
Whose lion-rage curbed by thick-ribbèd piles
Chafes on the pebbled strand. Stretching for miles
Her life-stream winds in robes of richest dyes,
When sunset gilds her palace, domes, and spires.
Behind, the broad green Downs support the skies,
Crowned with a wreath of clouds when day expires;
While from their ebon-throne veiled Night steps down,
Hushing the mighty life-voice of the town.

GOLDSTONE BOTTOM.

WHEN in a thoughtful mood, I often stray
Over the Downs into a grassy dell,
Where, on the banks that skirt the public way,
Blossom the bird's-eye and the pimpernel.
And there I stand, and watch the life-forms play
In the thick waters of a pond, where dwell
Newts, beetles, frogs, too numerous to tell,
Doomed to become the thoughtless schoolboy's prey.
Daisies and buttercups spangle the grass ;
The furze rich bloom, hanging like golden shells

Rifled by honey bees, I view, then pass
Up to the hedge of may, and hear the bells
Mellowed by distance echoing in the air,
As if blessed souls were holding converse there.

THE SOUTH DOWNS.

SWIFT-FOOTED Time with downy step has fled,
Ages on ages have been piled, life-dust
On dust, like book-leaves on this old world's crust,
Since God's creative hand these Downs outspread
In gentle undulations far and wide,
With crests, and vales, and coombes. How sweet to walk
Over the turf that shrouds life's ruins—chalk,
Formed at a thousand feet beneath the tide!
Broad-shouldered hills, yclad in living green,
Towering towards the sky that crowns your peaks,
How beautiful ye are in summer's sheen
When your health-breezes crimson lily cheeks!
Myriads of hearts, oh hills, have ceased to beat
Since heaven first kissed your heads and ocean bathed
    your feet!

A LIFE-PHASE.

I.

This sorrow-world of adder-stinging pain,
Pavèd with flints and glass that make us bleed,
Slew a fair angel once, whose word and deed
Welled from a pure and loving heart, whose brain
Was the rich palace of thought's royal king!
Full twenty years have vanished, love, since I—
Conning the lessons of soul-wisdom high—
Sat by thy bed of pain and suffering;
And there we vowed, who left this world of grief
Should to the other come and bring relief.
That promise has been kept, for from thy throne,
When stern affliction fires my throbbing brow,
Thou dost descend and comfort—thou, alone,
Sweet monitress of heaven, art with me now.

II.

Thou wert the only friend I ever had,
Whose influence was like the blessèd spring,
Breathing life's essence into everything;
Rousing the ice-bound earth with laughter glad;
Filling with sunshine the dark soul within.
Thus, from my heart, didst thou bring good from bad :

But when clear streams of kindness from it welled,
Sweetly they flowed, till soiled by inky sin.
From Wisdom's rule, my passions strong rebelled,
And, like a viper, stung thee for thy pains.
Oh, suffering martyr, when death burst thy chains,
And led thee, sainted virgin, into heaven,
No sorrow-floods could then wash out my stains!
Mercy, sweet spirit! Say, "Thou art forgiven."

III.

From the soul-sphere a lovely spirit's fleeing,
Arrayed in garments like the new-fallen snow;
Bringing sweet mercy's sunshine-streams, that flow
Into my heart, and rill through all my being!
She lays her hand upon me, whispering low,
"Arise, afflicted spirit, from the dust,
For mercy rids thee of the hellish brood
That dog the footsteps of ingratitude.
Hope be thy life-star—angels love the just!
The seven-fold heated furnace has been passed;
Sweet sorrow purifies, when the keen blast
Of grief is gone. Trust in thy God: arise!"
Almena spake, then gently on me cast
A radiant smile, and vanished in the skies!

SONNETS AND POEMS COMPOSED IN 1860.

PROGRESSION.

OH come, sweet spirit, faithfully pourtray
The mental moods through which I daily pass;
Catch the fleet shadows as they cross the glass,
And photograph the same. Life is not play,
But stern reality. We must work alway;
For see the beasts, the insects, flowers, and grass,
Improve their time; and shall our God-like class,
That bears a higher rank, do less than they?
God's Book is open. Nature, mother dear!
With pointed finger, bids us read a page.
Progression is the spirit of the age;
And we must do her bidding. Oh, how clear
Her darkest problems are unto the sage,
Who, with the sun of thought, lights up her mystery
    sphere.

CHARLES SIENKIEWICZ, THE POLISH POET AND HISTORIAN.

OBIIT FEBRUARY 7TH, 1860.

THE reaper's Death; humanity, the corn
That falls before his sickle-edge so keen!
This life is but a shadow's shade, a scene
That quickly shifts, like a light-flooding morn
Into a cloud-black night, of beauty shorn.
The world is now what it has ever been,
And lordly man, as soon as he is born,
Becomes Death's prey, who claims him as his own.
Great souls have wandered from us to the shore
Of that bright spirit-land; but not alone,
For angels were their guides. Oh, never more
Shall patriot-Pole hang on the accents rich
Of him who kept strict guard before the throne
Of freedom's God, immortal Sienkiewicz!*

* Pronounced "Senkyvich."

SEAFORD.

INSCRIBED TO HENRY SIMMONS, ESQ.

I.

Thou dear old town! where first I saw the light,
Nestled 'neath hills within a noble bay;
Where, still as death, the wind-bound vessels lay,
Sheltered by cliffs of alabaster white!
From Castle Green, how glorious is the sight
By land and sea! For miles the billows play,
Crowning the bow-like strand with wreaths of spray,
Backed by the distant hills, whose highest flight
The blue sky caps. Thy harbour is no more;
Beach-smothered now, though famed in days of yore
When England's Cinque-port navy ruled the flood,
Manned by the Vikings brave, who battles won,
Charters and rights, and sealed them with their blood.
King-gifts! treasured and handed down from sire to son!

II.

THE CLIFFS.

Oh, how sublime, how awful, are these cliffs,
That from the sea shoot upward to the sky,

Casting their shadows o'er the passing skiffs,
Stooping to catch the billows' mournful cry!
The fisher seems a speck amid the foam
That decks the beach with beauteous fringe of snow;
While voice of man and ocean from below
Are faintly heard. Here sea-gulls find a home,
Wheeling in mid air down the steep descent;
And on a jutting crag the ravens sit;
While high o'er all the screaming falcons flit,
Stilling the din of jackdaws' parliament.
Ye cliffs! companions of the storm, of yore
Were not your giant-forms fashioned 'neath ocean's roar?

III.

THE DOWNS.

The downs are studded o'er with flocks of sheep,
The close-cropped grass assumes a livelier hue,
The gold furze blossoms and the heath-buds peep
Above the tufts. Hyacinths, pink and blue,
Ere the sun rises, sip the morning dew,
And wild thyme scents the fresh and bracing air.
The linnet warbles on the wind-rocked spray:
Hither, in summer's prime, wheatears repair,

And in turf-traps become the shepherd's prey.
In Puck Church parlour lives yon aged pair
Of jet-black ravens, there they build their nest,
And issue forth to sound the sick man's knell.
While rabbits sport in yonder quiet dell,
Where Roman warriors in their stone urns rest!

IV.

THE CHURCHYARD.

Here, by the church, beneath this grassy sod,
In peace the ashes of my sires repose.
And here may I, when my weak eyelids close,
At last find rest. Upon their graves, my God,
I humbly kneel; and in Thy mercy trust
That Thou wilt spare to me this blessèd sight—
To see Thy glorious works, in them delight.
Fear not, my soul, for though thy mansion's dust,
Yet thou immortal art! Ye sweet bells, peal!
That once so merrily rang for those who sleep,
As 'tis not fit a bridal pair should weep
For the cold dead! Your notes, like voices, steal,
Mirthful and sad, as generations pass,
Lightly to tread upon or lie beneath the grass.

LOVE OF NATURE.

Up, and be joyful! for the day is ours;
Bright shines the sun, sweet is the balmy air!
The bee is on the wing, the leaves and flowers
With mirth are dancing; joy is everywhere!
Sweet sing the birds, the timid rabbit scours
Across the plain, and startles plovers there;
While sun and rain, that life-productive pair,
Make the earth gay. Let others pass their hours
In populous cities mid smoke and gloom,
While I with flowers in the gay fields will bloom,
Watching sweet Nature with a thoughtful look;
Get from her wondrous pages all I can,
Well knowing hers to be the wisest book
To study in, and learn to be a man!

TO SOME EARLY VIOLETS.

Glad messengers that tell us Spring is coming,
Sweet scented violets bathed in crystal dew;
Peering with modest eyes into the blue
And smiling heavens! Ye come ere bees are humming

Their monotone, after the thrush is heard;
A short time ere the cuckoo, or the bird
That brings his love-song from a fiery clime.
Ye tell glad tidings, violets; though no word
Escapes your lips, you speak in thoughts sublime
Of hallowed Freya! Why cower ye 'neath the grass
Upon the green bank-sides; or seek to shun
The large bright eye of the All-Father Sun,
Who makes your grace and beauty far surpass
Those of a blooming bride, and she the loveliest one?

THE DYKE.

On the steep summit of the Dyke I stand,
Gazing with wonder on the scene below,
The beauteous Weald, where silver streamlets flow
Through wood and mead the loveliest of the land!
Here stood the Celt, and here his Roman foe
Has left the traces of his skilful hand,
Near this deep Dyke, so marvellously planned,
Wrought by the mighty flood-rush long ago,
Since a great river through the Wealden dashed,
And monstrous creatures in its waters splashed!

Ye fair green hills, that they have withstood the storms
Of the rude elements that round you fly;
Age bows you not, proudly your giant-forms
Stand as they stood when first they kissed the sky!

A PLEA FOR THE POOR.

I.

WHY should the poor despair? To them is given
A dower of hope richer than golden ore;
God sorely tries them; many a heart He's riven,
And pierced with grief, stabbed to the very core.
Such is the fate of all souls bound for heaven.
Though world-despised, yet "blessèd are the poor."
Give then, ye rich, from your abundant store;
That mercy, God's best gift, may on you fall,
Like summer dew upon the thirsty flowers;
That in the awful gloom of your last hours
The spirits of the poor may light the road
You all must go, with faith-torch of St. Paul;
"Give to the poor that ye may lend to God,"
That angel-beggars' prayers may save you all!

II.

The air is sharp, the frost is everywhere;
In these hard times, pity the suffering poor!
Sparrows with ruffled plumes come to your door
For a few crumbs; yet beggars harder fare
Beneath a hedge; for, starving, should they dare
To ask for bread, in gaol they would deplore
Their bitter lot! Oh, ye rich men, that store
Your heads with law, but strip your hearts so bare
Of Christian love, praise God both night and day
That He has made you better off than they;
That you were not born beggars,—do not wince :
For had He willed yon ragged boy to be
Your own dear child, a noble, or a prince,
How different his sad lot! Then give him charity!

III.

Born in the dens of vice, in misery bred,
Is it a wonder lovely women sin?
Or hug the social evil that we dread,
Maddened by suffering and the demon—Gin?
In homes like theirs can virtue enter in;
Where vice and misery their infections spread,

And venom-fever fires the aching head
Till the brain reels, and horrid spectres grin?
Pity their sins, ye judges, spare the rod!
Better for them had they been never born;
Worse housed and fed than dogs; the scoff and scorn
Of their good sisters, who have always trod
The velvet paths of life! How sad, forlorn,
Are the poor Magdalenes, pitied by none save God!

LINES

WRITTEN IN A FIELD BEFORE THE HOUSE IN WHICH MY FATHER DIED.

AH, me! how swiftly do the years pass by!
In yonder house did my dear father die;
In this green field how often would I play,
Culling sweet flowers, whiling hours away.
The skylark's song, the spangled butterflies,
The chirping grasshopper and ants so wise;
Blue-wingèd flies on sorrel leaves so sour,
The honey-bee flitting from flower to flower,
The fearful field-mouse through the young grass creeping,
And yonder tiny child, with sorrow weeping,

To me recall my boyhood-time elysian :
'Tis beaming o'er me like a sainted vision,
Coming from dream-land, where in bliss it sleeps,
And in the past my whole existence steeps !

Old wrinkled Time has spread his sable wings,
And white-haired Sorrow in his sad train brings :
O'er the sweet past his night-black veil has thrown,
Which nought can pierce save memory alone.
Man falls like corn before the reaper, Death,
And soul and body part with vital breath :
All life is subject to decay, and—I
Must live a space, then with my fathers lie.
But ere this life-form mingles with the sod,
Or quits these fields which they have often trod,
Oh, grant, Celestial Father of this world,
Before in realms unknown my spirit's hurled,
That I some little good may do while here,
Trusting in Thee alone, and nothing fear !

See the cloud-shadows flit across the grass,—
How like to them, o'er earth, our shadows pass !
Singly we journey on, like winding streams,
Through varied landscapes to the land of dreams.

Behold yon skylark, quivering on his wings,
The higher up he soars the more he sings;
Fanning the air in the blue sky above,
Bursting his little heart with song of love,
Till, like a hawk, he drops within his nest:
Thus mount we up—alas! thus sink to rest.

God breathes a life-soul into all that lives,
And to the simplest flower rich perfume gives;
To man his wisdom, instinct to the beast,
Light to the stars, and does all Nature feast
With the good things of heaven, refreshing earth
With life renewed each Spring, as at her birth,
When the world's soul arose enlightening all;
When birds sang, beauty bloomed, and love did fall
Like summer dew upon the leaves and flowers;
When insects chirped among their grassy bowers,
And the first man awoke, a living soul,
Gazing with love and wonder on the whole!

Yes; beauty and love, and life and light, are new,
As at the world's first dawn; each blade I view
Springing, with wonder, from its parent sod,
Displays as much as man the hand of God!

Oh, listen to His voice which greets the ear,
Whispering sweet comfort—bids us never fear
Sin's demon-bands, which oft our minds assail,
But battle boldly, and we must prevail.
Then, ere our spirits burst life's prison bars,
And flit to happier homes in brighter stars—
Our spirit-mansions when this earth we've trod,
And left the mortal to become a clod—
Oh, let us wisely live and act the part
Of that God-Man who for our sins did smart:
Evil resist, and its hell-dooming power,
Then will our death be pure as life's first hour.

MARY.

I.

FAIR as the dawn, as dew-drop bright
   Sweeter than violet which uncloses
Its azure eyelids with delight;
   With cheeks betinged with bloom of roses!
Graceful and beauteous as the fawn
   That skips before the god of light,
With sunbeam-steps across the lawn,

Is my dear maiden lovely, slender !
   With lips of cherry-red, where bees
   Pilfer their honey-dew as fees,
Hiving among her cheek-bloom tender !—
   As saucy breeze in flower-cell dips
   Stealing perfume, so from her lips
May I sip love ! O God, defend her !

II.

I'll buy my love a cottage cosy,
   And plant a plot her soul to please
   With choicest flowers and rarest trees,
And there will pluck the prettiest posy,
   And give to her on bended knees,
   In singing love's rich melodies,
Till o'er her cheeks the blushes rosy
   Do blossom like a field of peas !
My love is fair, and tall, and young,
With hazel eyes and silver tongue,
And marble forehead broad and high !
   Wee feet and ankles ; shape so slim ;
   With features of a cherubim
Who's fallen, like love, from yonder sky !

III.

And thus we'll love and live together,
 'Mong flowers, and birds, and trees, and streams,
In laughing spring and summer weather,
 And winter pass in golden dreams,
With our song-spirits, light as feather,
 Yet full of thought as golden beams
 Of May's life-sun, when old earth teems
With wisdom-flowers, which poets gather
 And weave rich chaplets for the brows
 Of their beloved! Then when the boughs
Of golden-tinted fruit-trees swing,
 When sheep are bleating to the fold,
 And earth and ocean steeped in gold,
This love-song to my love I'll sing!

LOVE-SONG.

In love's first dawn I fondly thought
 A brown-cheeked girl a perfect fairy;
But th' ideal which long I sought
 I found in none but thee, my Mary!

Thy graceful form, bright hazel eyes,
  Sweet lips outvying rose or cherry!
Dark curls that shade a brow so wise,
  With truthful loving heart so merry!

Sweet pearly mouth where kisses bloom
  In dewy freshness like moss roses,
When life starts up from winter's tomb,
  When June his sun-bright eye uncloses.

Thy voice is tuneful as the tongue
  Of nightingale when he sings darkling;
When earth is green and May is young,
  Embodying flowers like diamonds sparkling.

The sheep bleat on the daisied turf,
  The green world grows, the bees are humming,
The hawthorn blossoms white as surf,
  The cuckoo sings, and summer's coming!

Then let us wander through the dells,
  And in the meads where cows are lowing:
Or, o'er the hills and pluck blue-bells,
  For God-life in each form is flowing!

Love universal is the theme :
  Dewdrops and sun-beams kiss the flowers,
Trees, shrubs, and grass from winter's dream
  Leap up to meet electric showers !

Then let us from our cottage stray ;
  Eve lowers her veil, the daisy closes,
The glowworm lights his silver ray,
  And Day on couch of flowers reposes !

Oh, Mary, hazel-eyed, how sweet
  To hold within my hand thy fingers !
To feel love's thrill when glances meet,
  Like sweetest notes of God's best singers !

What is it makes me tremble so ?
  'Tis love's electric shock of feeling ;
Through every pore his fire-flames glow,
  O'er brain, through nerves and arteries stealing.

Oh, happy love ! Oh, merry birds !
  That build and sing around our dwelling !
Oh, winds and streams, that whisper words
  Of love divine, from old earth welling !

Oh, Mary, thou the fountain art,
  From which is rilling all my pleasure ;
Enthroned thou sitt'st within my heart,
  Life's richest gem, earth's choicest treasure !

HELEN.

DEAREST Helen, let me sip
Love's sweet honey from thy lip.
More refreshing than the dew,
Food of men and angels too !
Let your smiles in bubbles rise
From your heart-fount to your eyes ;
Where I gaze as in a lake
Till their deepness makes me quake ;
Where my baby self I view
Mirrored in a heaven of blue.
Lightly tread, my lady sweet ;
Flowers court your pretty feet ;
At their light touch gaily rise,
Nod their heads, and ope their eyes ;
Breathe around you rich perfume,
Blushing laugh and brighter bloom !

Birds of song your presence hail;
When you walk in grove or vale
Saucy breezes rush to meet you,
Forest trees bow down to greet you.
Everything, my charming creature,
Loves you, as I love each feature
Of that pretty face so sly,
Where the rose and lily vie;
Where the rich carnation tips
Down of cheeks and luscious lips;
Where twin rows of teeth are spread,
Ivory white, 'twixt cherry red;
Where your tongue gives birth to words
Sweeter than the notes of birds;
Where your breath, a rich perfume,
Makes your face with blushes bloom!
Graceful Helen! peer of girls!
Cupid lurks among your curls;
Hides in dimples of your chin;
Or, in eyelids plotting sin,
Often from his love-lair starts;
In your glance his arrow darts,
Shoots and wounds me unto death,
·Till revived by kisses' breath!

Lying wounded at your feet,
Have compassion on me, sweet!
Let love-glances of your eyes
(Twin stars stolen from yonder skies)
Fall upon me like sun-ray,
Waking up the new-born day.
You can cure what is amiss
With a life-reviving kiss.
Let us, then, place mouth to mouth ;
Breathe upon me like the south
Soft wind, that flits from roses
When the eye of morn uncloses.
Then I'll drain the cup divine,
Overflowing with love's wine,
To the dregs, and pledge thee mine,
Till in ecstasies I swim,
Maiden child of cherubim !

THE SEASONS.

SPRING.

Spring's lovely mantle falls upon the earth,
Studded with life-forms, robed in gorgeous dyes :
The very air breathes love ! the sun, the skies,
And golden morn are fresh, as at their birth;
While bud and leaf and flower are issuing forth
With sweetest music from the throats of birds
And the light footfall of the showers, which pass
O'er hill and dale, gemming the young green grass
With cowslips and daisies rare ! Flocks and herds
And the green world now feel the breath of Spring ;
The very dust is life upon the wing ;
And earth, rebaptized by the blessèd rain,
Grows joyous as a child whose accents ring
This merry peal, "The cuckoo's come again ! "

SUMMER.

The golden mantled Summer, crowned with flowers,
Comes from the sunny south to our dear isle,
Gilding the emerald leaves ! While her sweet smile

Gladdens the earth, whom she profusely dowers
With the life-gift of warm productive showers!
Breathes her rich bloom on fruit; rewards the toil
Of those who labour hard to make the soil
Yield a rich harvest. Up the blue welkin towers
The sprightly lark, till like a speck he's seen
At heaven's gate. The rail crakes mid the green
And blooming corn; gnats sport, the wild bees hum;
The mower whets his scythe; sheep cluster on the hill;
The cattle pant; the nightingale is still,—
And earth is gorgeously arrayed, now Summer's come!

AUTUMN.

The luscious Autumn, apple-cheeked and merry,
Like a rich farmer, walks among the corn
Standing in golden sheaves, and sees it borne
Home on the wains and stored; when the dewberry
And orchard fruits are ripe, and huntsman's horn
Rings tally-ho! while robin, red as cherry,
Greets with his simple song the ruddier morn;
And vats o'erflow with cider, beer, and perry;
When the sweet birds have flown across the seas

To other climes; when leaves fall from the trees,
And fields are bare, and harvest feast is given,—
Then Autumn, trembling at the Winter's birth,
Grows sad and dies; and from her grave, the earth,
Soars like a blessèd soul, to rest in heaven!

WINTER.

Teeth-chattering Winter, with his snowy hair
And wrinkled face, striding a northern blast,
Came howling by.   Earth shuddered as he passed,
Her limbs grew rigid, and her features fair;
Sap fled, leaves whirled, birds died, and the sharp air
Did tremble with the cold.   Anon there crept
A death-chill o'er the Earth, who, shrieking loud,
Gave up the ghost on Winter's snowy shroud,
While tears of ice adown his rough cheeks swept.
As change the seasons, so man lives and dies;
Emblem of bud and flower, sunshine and cloud.
Till death's good angel comes to heal his pain,
Closes his eyes in sleep, to wake again
In the bright spirit-world which round us lies!

ROSA.

I.

I KNOW a pretty rose-bud maiden !
Oh, may she ne'er be sorrow laden,
   Nor droop when life-showers on her fall !
For she is truthful, loving, merry,
And tempting as the luscious cherry
   That peeps thro' leaves by the garden wall.
I'm summer-ripe, while she's a bud
Unfolding into womanhood ;
     The peer of girls,
     With waving curls,
   And two black eyes outsparkling all !

II.

When grey-eyed dawn pale light is shedding,
Through pearly dew her way she's treading,
   In the valleys, among the corn,
To see the laughing flowers a-springing,
And early larks to heaven a-winging,
   With merry song to hail the morn.
I'm summer-ripe, while she's a bud

Unfolding into womanhood ;
    The peer of girls,
    With waving curls,
Whom all admire, and none can scorn !

III.

Upon her face sweet smiles have motion
Like the sun-kissed waves of ocean,
    Diamond-crested by the breeze.
Thought-buds in her mind a-blooming
Show a golden harvest coming
    Richly laden like the bees !
I'm summer-ripe, while she's a bud
Unfolding into womanhood ;
    The peer of girls,
    With waving curls,
Crowned with the bloom of orchard trees.

IV.

Earth, sea, and sky are golden tinted,
And Summer's lovely face is printed
    On fruits that love the garden wall ;
Apple and plum, and peach cheeked rosy,

With August flowers that deck her posy;
But this sweet maid outvies them all;
I'm summer-ripe, while she's a bud
Unfolding into womanhood;
    The peer of girls,
    With waving curls,
May God's rich blessings on her fall!

GOD'S PIONEERS.

YE men of thought and action, who ne'er shirk
The noble duties God has on you laid,
What though you're world-despised and badly paid,
God's pioneers are you and do His work;
While we, like bigot-priests, behind you lurk,
And at the bugbear Doubt shrink back afraid,
You onward bravely march, and undismayed,
Grapple the devil—beard him like a Turk!
Bold Thought and Doubt, twin brothers, rule the world;
By them is Truth set free, and Falsehood hurled
Back to its home of everlasting night;
While Knowledge, foot-tracked by the angel Worth,

Darkness dispels with its all-radiant light,
And God's bright heaven of love prepares to dawn on earth !

INDEPENDENCE.

I AM not prone to flatter for a crust,
Or bait with gilded lies to fish for praise !
What though I never wear a crown of bays,
Shall I debase the man, crawl, lick the dust,
And flatter wealth, or make the bright soul rust
Into its core by singing canting lays ?
Why should I laud a slave, whose nights and days
Are spent in hoarding treasures which he must,
In dying, leave to some expectant friend ?
The soul, for peace, must on herself depend—
Work out her own salvation—crush the lust
That lures her from her God. How can the slave
Of all that's earthly ever hope to rise
Into the sphere where dwell the good and wise,
Burst through the bonds of death, and triumph o'er the grave ?

WRITTEN DURING A SEVERE ILLNESS.

I.

WHAT agonizing pains like lightning dart
Along the thought-ways leading to the brain,
As if life's silver cords were rent in twain !
The sun's blessed beams that ought to cheer my heart
Thrust in my eye-balls daggers tipped with pain.
How the weak nerves do tremble, throb, and start,
Stretched to their full extent, then back rebound !
The brain's on fire, sight fails, the strong limbs bow,
And the poor body's prostrate on the ground.
The human mechanism, at work till now,
Stops like a run-down watch ; the great mainspring,
The wonder-coil, is broken or unwound ;
And e'en the soul, that most mysterious thing,
Droops with the body ; when it's hale, is sound !

II.

O Lord my God, how weak, how sad, am I !
The strong limbs bow and tremble like a leaf ;
My pulse beats quick, I'm feverish, give relief ;
For though alone I feel that THOU art nigh !

To THEE in all my agony I cry ;
To THEE pour forth my sorrow and my grief;
Oh, purify this heart, and let my chief
And richest thoughts mount to THY throne on high !
Without THEE, what is man ? A shadow's shade—
A thought that flits before in words arrayed.
Hide not the sunshine of THY face, but give
Pardon for all my sins ; let them be hid
Behind THY mercy-veil. Oh, make me live
A better life, to do what THOU may'st bid !

A CHRISTIAN GENTLEMAN.

A THOROUGH English gentleman I know,
From whose rich mind pure streams of virtue flow,
Clear and transparent as from mercy's fount,—
A follower of HIM who, on the Mount,
Preached love and righteousness, and blessed the poor,
And sent His angel, Peace, from door to door.
He clothes the naked, gives the hungry food,
Lives out a Christian life in doing good ;
Gives homes to orphan girls of friends bereft ;
And what his right hand does hides from his left.

He seeks the burdens of the poor to lighten,
And is a blessing to the town of Brighton.
A noble patriot he, whose rich blood curds
At cruel acts; a man of deeds, not words;
Humble and modest, full of sense and worth,
And, though but man, does angel-deeds on earth!
Than whom there is not in our mother-isle
A gentleman more free from pride or guile;
Whose conscience, mirror-like, reflects the truth;
Who, hating sin, has for the sinner ruth;
Worships one God alone; is no sectarian;
But loves an honest Catholic or Arian.
Prayers on his head, like dews of summer fall;
For, as a man and friend, he's loved by all.
When knave's exploits are trumpet-blown by fame,
Oh Muse, be wise, and hide this good man's name!

TO MARK ANTHONY LOWER, ESQ., F.S.A.

THOU gold-thought diver in the Sea of Ages,
Bringing rich treasures to the world of light,
Gemmed with rare brilliants set in facets bright,
Sparkling like stars upon thy lucid pages!

Pleasing instructor, oh, with what delight
We glean, through thee, great deeds of ancient sages!
Thou from the past uplift'st the veil of night,
Showing us "merrie England" once again,
With feudal castles, knights clad gorgeously,
With banners of the antique chivalry,
Binding our Saxon-land with iron chain.
Then Lower, themes of humbler life are thine,
While wit drops sparkling from thy pen like rain,—
God bless thy pleasant work, searcher in wisdom's mine!

MAY.

I.

THE buds are bursting into leaf on trees,
And May's warm breath is rousing everything;
The songs of nightingales float on the breeze,
And with the cuckoo's solo welcome spring.
Cowslips and buttercups in meadows bloom;
The crimson-tinted daisy opes its eye.
The painted lady bursts her winter-tomb,
And with the humble-bee sports in the sky.

The streamlets sparkle in the gold sunshine,
The dewdrops glisten on the new-born grass;
The skies are smiling with a face divine,
While the life-cycles through their changes pass;
From seed to seed they haste, with life to death,
Roused by sweet May, slain by December's breath.

II.

MORNING.

The crimson-blushing rose hangs on the thorn
While dewdrops sparkle on its velvet leaves;
From sea of fire up shoots the young May morn:
The robin chirps, birds twitter 'neath the eaves,
And from his new-made nest among the corn
The skylark mounts and sings. The fair twilight
Kisses the eyelids of the sleeping flowers
That open, smile, and tremble with delight!
The purple violet 'neath the green grass cowers,
Extracting rich perfume from air and showers,
Which south winds pilfer with a fond embrace.
Woodland and vale to matin hymns give birth,
While nature rises with a smiling face,
And hails the loving Sun the bridegroom of the Earth!

III.

EVENING.

What crimson bars, what gold-flakes streak the skies !
How still the air ! how peaceful is the earth !
The heaveless ocean in soft slumber lies,
And lovely flowers, which the fair morn brought forth
Now close their dewy lids. Starlight is streaming
Through the dim veil that shrouds the face of day,
And the sweet infant Spring in happy dreaming
Is lulled to rest. The full-orbed moon is beaming,
Shedding her silver light on leaf and spray,
And the lone bird begins his heavenly lay,
To which all Nature listens ! Night-winds creep
With silent footfall through the young green leaves
Fearing to rouse a whisper. Calm in sleep
Earth's spirit lies ; her bosom scarcely heaves !

A *SOUTH-DOWN SKETCH.*

I.

THE COTTAGE.

Beneath the Downs, in a most pleasant spot,
Stands a thatched cottage, where the eglantine
And monthly roses round the door entwine,
With honeysuckle and forget-me-not !
To cool the warm air when the summer's hot,
Around the small-paned window trails the vine
With its plump grapes. Nature and art combine
To make a fairy palace of this cot !
Garden and orchard robe in gorgeous hues ;
On the fruit-laden boughs the birds are merry ;
The red-cheeked apple, plum, and ruddier cherry,
Ripen in golden sunshine, which imbues
The peach, the apricot, and nectarine,
With a pink-purple bloom, flushing their leaves rich
    green !

II.

THE ORCHARD.

Within this orchard, 'neath an apple-tree,
When the sweet-brier, the violet, and moss-rose

Perfume the air, ere the day's eyelids close,
I stretch me on the grass, and hear with glee
The garden warbler sing right lovingly,
To his dear mate, his own melodious woes,
While golden roseate tints the sunset throws
On sky and cloud and on the deep blue sea.
When all is silent save the voiceful bird,
When not a rustle 'mong the leaves is heard,
When night's veil falls, and bat and owl come forth,
I gaze into the blue serene above,
And see bright angels visit this old earth,
And hush her soul asleep with lullaby of love !

III.

THE DAY'S DEATH AND BIRTH.

How still she lies ! Another day is dying ;
An icy shudder creeps through everything :
Nor bat nor muffled owl is on the wing,
And not a sound is heard, except the sighing
Of the old day, in his keen death-throes lying.
Oh, close his eyes, for he is dead ! The spring
Of the new day has dawned. Hills, valleys ring
As he on golden plume is westward flying,

Bidding the breeze and choristers to sing
His glorious birth, and hail him as their king !
Day springs from night, and life's the fruit of death,
Ages to ages tell the same old story :
Flesh dies, and gives to flesh its vital breath,
But mind for ever lives in all its glory.

MORNING.

To paint the Morn in all her hallowed glory,
Go forth into the fields before the sun
Streaks the blue sky with purple cloud-flakes gory,
Ere the rich song of nightingale's begun,
Or dew-drop-world, suspended on the leaf,
Kissed by its sunbeam-lover, fades away ;
When darkness steals on tiptoe like a thief
Adown the western sky ; when golden day,
With wings of light, flits over mount and flood,
And the young daisy opes its milk-white bud ;
When soft winds breathe, leaves stir, and cattle low,
And the whole world, refreshed, starts up from sleep,
While in her veins life-streams from heaven flow,
And matin-hymns burst forth, rich toned and deep.

TO WENTWORTH HOLWORTHY, ESQ.

ABROAD into the fields ! nor longer mope
In deep abstraction in your book-filled room ;
For the bright sun's dispelled a week of gloom :
Take with you Chaucer and your microscope ;
For life's awake, and the wee flowrets bloom
Under the grass, lovely of rainbow hues.
Here's a gem ! a gossamer steeped in dews,
Hanging like silver veil on budding broom.
God's work of wonder everywhere is seen—
In air, in water, and the world of green ;
Germs feel His breath and start up into life.
Gaze through the microscope upon this leaf :
Another world's revealed, where it is rife,
Joyful and sad as in our own, but, oh, how brief !

I.

STIR up the mind within you ! Do not rust ;
The world has need of earnest men and true.
Why should a brother, grovelling in the dust,
Cry out for help and be refused by you ?
Do a good deed, and that you'll never rue !
For there's a God above, who loves the just,

No matter what their creed : and those that trust
With a brave heart in Him, He will guide through
This stormy world into his peaceful heaven.
Rise from thy slumber! Unto thee is given
A dower of love and genius. Use it, then,
For the world's good ; pay interest with the loan ;
Scatter the seed among thy brother-men :
They'll till the soil,—the harvest be thine own.

II.

CRINGE not, fawn not, lie not, though you be
As poor and wretched as a beggar born ;
Love God and Truth, spite of the fool's scorn,
Nor let world-fashion make a slave of thee.
That man is Freedom's son, whose thought is free
As the pure air he breathes ; who, left forlorn,
'Reft of his all, still like a glorious morn
Peers through the mist and shines resplendently !
Tyrants may kill the body, but the soul,
Like wind and wave, stoops not to their control.
Falsehood in pomp may dazzle for a time,
But truth in simple majesty will beam,
On men who'll wake as from a monstrous dream,
And the death-knell of superstition chime.

III.

THE world has great and good men still alive,
Who do their work in silence, watch and pray
For that blessed time when truth shall reign for aye,
And love be God's rich dower—souls that strive
Against their lower nature, and derive
Help from above their passions to allay.
Of those who conquer self, God is the stay;
He does not leave them—in good deeds they thrive.
Yet sad's the fate of those great souls indeed,
Who carry out the precepts of our creed,—
"Do unto others as ye would that they
Should do to you;" for though they're good and wise
The world hates truth, and fondly hugs its lies,
Hunting God's seers to death like savage beasts of prey.

CHRISTMAS EVE.

THE earth beneath her snowy shroud is sleeping;
The skeleton trees, like ghosts, are robed in white;
While in a silver veil of moonbeams, steeping
The town in glory's flood-light, comes the night!

The waits and bells are carolling with delight,
And melodise the air with joyful sound ;
Hailing the blessèd morn of Jesus' birth,
Who left His heaven that love might here abound.
Stir up the fire : come, draw your chairs around ;
Tell cheerful tales ; drink the red wine, till mirth
And joy shake hands. The mistletoe's white berry
Vies with the holly's clustering beads of coral,
Heraldic symbols of old Yule-tide merry,
Who comes with jovial face, snow-crowned and decked
 with laurel !

THE SEA.

DEEP in thy crystal mirror do I gaze,
See sun and sky and cloudlet imaged there ;
Thou world's great eye, that upward with amaze
Look'st fondly into heaven. The loving air
Sweetly enfolds thee with a mother's care ;
Stormed into rage she lashes up thine own,
Cresting the billows with their wreaths of spray,
Whistling sad dirges to thy monotone.
What worlds of life in thy blue waters stray !

Image of Heaven! Scorner of Time! O Sea,
Ages have fled, since the Almighty's hand
Unleashed the winds and set thy billows free,
To wall around this happy, hallowed land,
Trod by a noble race, whose watchword's LIBERTY!

Could Poets turn a penny as a rhyme,
The world would worship them: for a rich purse
Now makes the gentleman, though he be worse
Than a rude boor; and poverty's a crime
Of such a dye, that if God's Son, sublime,
Could walk this earth, He'd rue the bitter curse
That clings to it. We preach that Gospel-verse
Blessing the poor, and curse them all the time.
What hypocrites we are to one another!
Ape honesty and truth, to cheat a brother;
And say we love, believe, what we despise.
No longer let us simulate, but be
What we profess, true men, and this life free
From that which darkens it—a cloud of lies!

TO THE WORKING-MEN OF BRIGHTON.

MEET is it sometimes you should hear the truth,
When *gentlemen* you're styled throughout the land ;
He was your Friend, ye Workers of the Hand,
Who called you "Brother-Men!" on you had ruth,
And scorned to flatter when, in vig'rous youth,
Your true position you 'gan understand
To think and rule yourselves, a social band,
Bent to exterminate "the unwashed, uncouth"!
Why have you left the moral paths you trod,
Fearless of scorn, strong in your Faith and God,
To slander your best friends? Is manhood dead,
Or grovelling in you? Up from the dust, and soar
To that high moral sphere where you of yore
Were NOBLEMEN, though toiling for your bread !

TO GOLD WORSHIPPERS.

LABOUR's a blessing, idleness a curse,
In this scheme-loving, good-bad world of ours;
Then let our aim be high, though Fortune showers

Her favours on the bad ; and what is worse,
Oft, like a highway robber, steals the purse
Of the good man, and, blind as Cupid, dowers
The base and sordid. Must good men mingle
With those whose brains within their pockets jingle,
Whose creed is "money makes the man"?—the swine
That trample on rich pearls, with souls of ink,
Who grope in darkness in the Devil's mine,
Haunted by ghosts of truth, yet from them shrink ?
Go, plunge in streams of love and mercy pure,
Which, like Bethesda's Pool, will work your cure !

BRIGHTON RACE HILL.

I.

A SIGHT more beautiful there cannot be
Than that which strikes the eye upon this Down.
Along the vale, up the hill's-sides, the town
Basks in the golden sunset gorgeously ;
While miles away, over the crested sea,
Of sky and cloud, wearing a purple crown,
Looms the fair isle, whose cliffs on ocean frown.

When o'er this velvet turf swift horses flee
In an exciting race, fair women, men,
Up the steep hill in crowds assemble then,
With happy faces, robed in rich array.
Here stands the hill, as from its birth it's stood :
But all the souls that since have swelled the flood
Of human life upon it—where are they?

II.

Echo repeats the question, but in vain ;
The sybil Nature's silent on this theme :
The present's real, the past is but a dream,
An unembodied thought that haunts the brain,
As in some melody a witching strain.
Oft as I musing watch a purling stream
Pursue its winding course, I sadly deem
That such is life flowing towards death's main !
Night spreads her sable wings, and Sleep comes down
With finger on his lip, and stills the town.
How sound it slumbers ! Not a whisper's heard,
As in deep thought I wander down the hill.
Where are the souls of man, of beast and bird,
When in thy arms, O Sleep ! their forms are still ?

III.

How marvellous is Sleep, whose healing balm
Pours in the frame new life at each day's close!
Go in the garden, watch the lovely rose
Fold up its leaves, and hear the vesper-psalm
Of the sweet nightingale, when all is calm
And the far west with rich vermilion glows;
And there you'll see, when night her mantle throws
Over the earth, blessed Sleep usurp her realm,
And in soft slumber every life-form steep.
Death is a wondrous mystery; so is Sleep:
Riddles which none can solve! Thy power I feel,
Queen of the silent night, soother of sorrow;
Come in thy loveliest shape, my senses steal,
Nor give them back, sweet spirit, till to-morrow.

SONNETS AND POEMS WRITTEN IN 1861.

TO JOHN ROBERTSON, ESQ.

May, with her gorgeous mantle, richly studded
With spring's sweet flowers, tinged with every hue,
Greens fields and hedge. The monarch oak has budded,
And this old marvellous earth is clothed anew.
While yonder, quivering in the cloudless blue,
The lark pours down his song, till earth is flooded
With waves of music. Leave your studies now,
And tread the Downs; ascend their topmost brow,
Where the life-breeze will strengthen thy weak frame,
And paint thy cheeks as ruddy as the cherry,
Or a young maiden's when she hears the name
Of her beloved. Away with care! Be merry
As yonder linnet warbling on the spray,
For the red lips of June touch those of May.

COUNTRY-LONGINGS.

OH, how I long to leave this din and noise !
To revel in the fields 'neath a blue sky ;
Or wander in the woodlands with my boys,
Teaching in Nature's school, where streams rush by,
Kissing green boughs that stoop to their embrace,
List'ning to Nature's sweet melodious voice !
Now the blue heavens put on a smiling face ;
My heart leaps up to meet them and rejoice !
Away, my soul ! revel among the flowers,
And breathe new life from sunshine and from showers !
No longer pine a captive in this room,
Wasting the body's health with mental toil,
Sowing rich knowledge in a stubborn soil,
To gain a paltry dole, mayhap an Otway's doom !

LIFE'S AUTUMN.

THE Summer of my life is fading now,
And Autumn's mournful dirge rings in mine ear,

While rugged wrinkles on my cheek and brow
Begin to whisper, Death and thou art near!
I loathe the pleasures that I once held dear.
My hair grows white, my limbs bend like the bough,
Eyes dim and memory fails, I know not how.
To leave this world, what makes me quake with fear?
The great unknown, the mystery-land, where death
Conducts the spirit, when he steals life's breath.
Wisdom is speechless by the awful grave,
And Science blind beyond this petty world.
We age, grow weak, and die, and then are hurled
Upon a shore whose name appals the brave.

HASTINGS.

INSCRIBED TO MESSRS. GEORGE AND FREDERICK EARP, WITH WHOM THE AUTHOR VISITED THE SCENES DESCRIBED.

I.

Thou old sea-town, crouching beneath the rocks
Like a strong lion waiting for his prey!
Where are thy river, harbour, and the docks
In which the navy of Old England lay?

Why didst thou slumber, when in Pevensey Bay
The Normans' mighty host profaned our soil,
When thou, the Cinque-Port Queen, didst hold the key
Which locked the sea-gates of this freedom-isle?
Why wert thou chartered, honoured, and made free
When all the land was manacled a slave?
Right loyal wert thou and thy seamen brave,
And Normen loved thee, as thou lov'dst the sea!
While all their foes, envying thy warlike fame,
Did fear thee, as, of old, they feared thy Viking-name!

II.

THE DRIPPING WELL.

'Neath a blue sky we stray, o'er hills, through dells,
And golden meads, by hedgerows, where blue-bells
And violets bloom, close to a rocky strand,
Fringëd with shrubs and flowers down to the edge
Of the blue sea! A nook of our dear land,
In which the rocks seem sundered by the wedge
Of giant-force, forming a lovely glen,

With Dripping Well, where the clear water rills,
Like silver threads, through the old sandstone hills,
Into a basin which o'erflows, and then
Steals with a voice of music from the ken,
Through tufted foliage, which the valley fills,
Dancing and gurgling, going where it wills,
Until it falls in Ocean like a sweet Amen!

III.

THE CASTLE HILL.

Here, on the sward, we lie, in feeling one;
Our mental lenses image all we've seen:
The gorgeous clouds of heaven, the earth's bright green,
Blue dimpled ocean, and the golden sun!
Eye-artists swift as thought before us run
Painting life-pictures o' the rainbow's sheen;
With castle, town, and bay, skiffs, towers, between
The eye and Beachy Head, shrouded in dun
And misty robes; while from his dark cloud-ledge
The sun steps down, and drives his golden wedge
Right through the heaving mass, which wingèd forms
Assume, light and fantastic as the spray,

Chased by the spirit-winds across the bay,
Till out the headland comes that braves the ocean storms!

WRITTEN UNDER GREAT MENTAL AFFLICTION.

I.

GOD's hand is heavy on me! Why, my heart,
Dar'st thou to murmur at His just decree?
For what He wills it is the best for thee,
Although He rend thee with His lightning-dart.
Grow strong in faith, and from the truth ne'er part,
However low in life thy lot may be.
Good men are bold, nor at Death's presence start,
But boldly face him when the wicked flee.
Oh, give me strength and courage, Lord, to bear
This weary burden life! Let not despair,
Or poverty, or fear, the talents rust
Which Thou hast given me. To Thee I pray
To dawn on my life-sphere a brighter day,
To raise me from affliction and the dust!

II.

The storm will soon burst o'er me,—how shall I
Stand up against its fury? Should I fall,
Uprooted, like the oak, majestic, tall,
Deserted by my God, how could I die?
Would, as a bird, I could from conscience fly,
That stings my soul, imprisoned in a wall
Of sinful flesh, to which it is the thrall!
Strike off its bonds, my God! Oh, hear my cry,
And guide me in the dubious course I run,
Groping in darkness dire; far from the sun
Of Thy bright face! Come, strengthen with Thy breath
My soul for this life-battle; so I can
Face friend or foe undaunted, like a man :
Be just and faithful even unto death!

THE MEW'S NEST SEEKER.

In the parish register of Seaford is the following entry :—" 1796, June 6th : Buried, John Cosstick, accidentally *killed by falling down the cliff* by endeavouring to take mews' eggs."

THE day was beautiful and fair,
    With joy the birds were singing ;
While, sweetly echoing in the air,
    The Sabbath bells were ringing.

Unto the church the good folks all
    With solemn steps were going,
Obedient to the sacred call
    That through the air was flowing.

When Cosstick left his humble cot,
    And up the hills went climbing
Until he reached the highest spot,
    And heard the church-bells chiming.

With one companion of his toil,
    The holy Sabbath breaking,
They drove the crow-bar in the soil,
    Then man and basket, shaking,

Over the cliff were gently swung
  To seek no costly treasure,—
For sea-mews' eggs he dangling hung
  'Twixt life and death, for pleasure.

Trembling and faint, high poised in air,
  His heart within him failing;
Four hundred feet below, and there
  The sea its dirge was wailing!

Mews o'er his head were wheeling round,
  The daws and falcons crying,
And ravens croaked, with dismal sound,
  The death-song of the dying.

The frail machine rocked to and fro,
  Flints cut the rope asunder,
He shrieked—he gazed above, below,
  Death-struck with fear and wonder!

Compressed in one short moment there,
  Life's dream was o'er him stealing;
And then his spirit winged the air,
  All rapture, sense, and feeling.

But down the cliff, with piercing yell,
  His wretched corpse went flying,
As the last tolling of the bell
  Upon the breeze came dying;

And crushed upon the shingle lay,
  Pale, mangled, without motion;
The only tears that bathed his clay
  Were those of weeping ocean!

Go! gaze, where oftentimes I've gazed,
  On those bold cliffs so hoary;
From ocean's base, look up, amazed,
  And picture this sad story!

———o———

SONGS WRITTEN IN 1862.

LILY BELLA.

LILY Bella, rosy Bella,
    Sylph with dangling curls,
Ivory teeth and laughing mouth,
    Most beautiful of girls.

Pretty Bella, dearest Bella,
    Sweet and kind and true,
I had a pleasant dream last night
    That we no more were two.

Graceful Bella, light-foot Bella,
    All my pleasure died,
When I woke and found that you
    Were not my loving bride.

Gentle Bella, pleasing Bella,
    A little word will bless,
And thrill through all my being :
    Do you love me? Whisper "yes!"

JEANETTE.

JEANETTE has reached meridian beauty,—
  She is a golden summer's day !
To whom my Muse must do her duty,
  And an admiring tribute lay
    Before the feet
    Of one so sweet,
So lovely, wise, so good and dear !
    If I were free
    Like honey bee,
I'd settle on her lips, and taste love's cheer !

Jeanette has blossomed like the roses,
  She is the queen of womanhood !
In speaking, her rich mind uncloses,
  And pours forth music like a flood !
    With fairy feet
    It ripples sweet
In angel-notes, rich, deep, and clear !
    If I were free
    Like honey bee,
I'd settle on her lips, and taste love's cheer !

Jeanette is queen of all my pleasure,
   Love's banneret doth o'er me wave!
Of all the world she is the treasure
   Which I most prize,—would be her slave!
     Like music dies
     In gushing sighs,
So her sweet voice I love to hear!—
     If I were free
     Like honey bee,
I'd settle on her lips, and taste love's cheer!

Jeanette will not be cruel hearted,
   But must forgive when love inspires!
Her soul-full eyes in me have darted
   Electric streams of heavenly fires,
     Which burn and blaze.
     At her love-gaze
I'm pleased, yet tremble when she's near.
     If I were free
     Like honey bee,
I'd settle on her lips, and taste love's cheer!

EMMA.

Emma, thou art merry;
    Pride of womanhood.
Cheek-bloom like the cherry,
    Lips of flesh and blood.

Lily neck, and bosom
    White as surf of sea;
Where sweet flowers blossom
    In love's vale for me.

Let me steal sweet kisses
    From thy rose-bud mouth;
Taste the rapturous blisses
    Of the loving south.

Now the summer's coming
    On her golden wings,
And the bees are humming
    Love-songs which she sings.

Kiss me, kiss me, ever;
    Kissing is divine;
I will Venus never
    Leave for god of wine.

Bee when sweets extracting
　Scarce in flower-cell dips ;
I'll be more exacting
　And drain love's cup,—thy lips !

MINNIE.

LITTLE winsome Minnie !
　She has pledged her word;
　　With her sweet breath,
　　To be till death
　My own sweet pretty bird !

Angel-featured Minnie !
　I to her will fly,
　　For she's the dove
　　I fondly love,
　And shall do till I die.

Open hearted Minnie !
　Merry, buxom, free ;
　　By night and day
　　We'll love and play,
　For she's the girl for me !

Blithesome, tempting Minnie,
    Tells me she is mine;
        And says she'll treat
        Me, when we meet,
    With kisses rich as wine.

Pretty graceful Minnie,
    Is a precious prize;
        She lights the fire
        Of my desire
    With her soul-sparkling eyes.

Pleasing, teasing Minnie!
    I will seek her nest;
        And there will sing,
        Like bird in spring,
    Woo, win, her, and be blest.

WINNIE.

    LITTLE Winnie's dove-like;
        Sky-blue are her eyes;
        Cheeks and lips of roses;
        Graceful, loving, wise.

Winnie has a cottage
    And garden, full of flowers,
Fencèd in with hedgerows,
    Rich in shady bowers.

Where a pretty goldfinch
    Sings a merry strain
'Mong the apple blossoms,
    And whiles away my pain.

Little Winnie listens;
    Tears stand in her eye;
I clasp her to my bosom,
    She heaves a gentle sigh.

Little Winnie pledges,
    In the leafy bowers,
She will be my love-wife,
    Sweeter than the flowers.

Winnie is an angel,
    Sent from heaven above,
To strew my path with roses,
    And fill my heart with love.

JENNY.

Jenny comes from Sylvan Worth,
    And is a winsome thing;
      She's neat and clean,
      And twice eighteen,
    Yet buxom as the spring.

Her lips are like the cherry,
    A-dangling on the tree;
      Her eyes are bright
      As starry night,
    Her teeth like ivory.

I love my dearest Jenny,
    I love her as my life;
      So kind and good
      For flesh and blood,
    My little precious wife!

Mary, Helen, Bella,
    Rosa, and Jeannette,
      Emma, Minnie,
      Little Winnie,
    Are all in Jenny met.

SONNETS AND POEMS WRITTEN IN 1868.

WAIL OF A BRUISED SPIRIT.

When first I woke, a spirit by the hair
Did on me seize, with inspiration fraught,
And plunge me headlong in the sea of thought,
That bubbles up its coruscations rare,
Illuming brilliantly the sphere of air
That girdles this God-world, in which I've wrought
With hand and brain, and fickle fortune sought,
But found instead poverty and despair!
Heart-broken, suffering from affliction's rod,
(Oh! what a world is this!) my lip-friends fly,
Like summer-birds when deathful winter's nigh,
And leave me desolate. Mercy, O God!
My life is grown so drear, I long to die;
Lift up my soul, bruised, broken, from this sod!

EPISTLE.

TO MARK ANTONY LOWER, ESQ., M.A., F.S.A.

To thee my gratitude, my love, belong;
To thee I dedicate a grateful song.
" I was an hungered, and you gave me bread;'
Sorrowing and sick, yet me you visited;
Cheered and consoled me, too, when lightning-pain
Did paralyse my limbs and stun my brain;
When poor and helpless on my bed I lay,
With life scarce pulsing in this house of clay,
Your pen's rich eloquence did a good deed,
Spoke like a friend, and proved *a friend* in need.
Up from the well of kindness which o'erflows
At the relation of another's woes,
The silver stream ran sparkling in the sun,
And in men's hearts it melted many a one
To pity and relieve me,—when the good God,
For some just cause, chastised me with His rod.
Oh, may the mercy and the bread which they
Cast on the waters, bless them every day!

My leal-tried friend, in sunshine and in shade,
In fame's gold Book thy name will never fade,
But brighter glow upon its dazzling pages,
As time unfolds its leaves to future ages.
Thou genial, learnèd man, kind, good withal,
Humour and wit, like sparkling dewdrops, fall,
Mingled with wisdom, from thy golden pen,
T' instruct and to amuse thy brother men!
Thy laughing, learnèd Muse, doth never rust;
Hoar-headed Eld, with heart as dry as dust,
And mummy-form, struck by the hand of death,
She animates with life's mysterious breath!
Thine is a pleasing, graceful, pliant Muse;
But mine is wilful, and doth oft refuse
To do my bidding; while thine, I wis,
Both a companion and a servant is.
My own's a saucy jade, that comes and goes,
Just as she pleases,—leads me by the nose,—
Makes me work hard in her excited fits,
Rouses my passions, captivates my wits;
Asleep, awake,—haunteth me everywhere,
Like a ghost-tune, at home, abroad, in prayer,
In sad, or merry moods;—and then departs,
Correctly named, the muse of fits and starts.

Would, by God's blessing, that you could inherit
A full-blown fortune, equal to your merit,
So that your labours in sweet peace might end!
Your country owes you much, my valued friend!
May the Queen send you, with a smile of pleasure,
A yearly cheque drawn on the nation's treasure.
Fortune, her ledger, with command to edit
The antiquarian relic to your credit!
Things, like the wind, would change then—men of letters
Become rich creditors, and not poor debtors;
Smaller returns fall in at every quarter,
To the aristocrats of bricks and mortar;
To money-grubbers, who out-Jew the Jew!
Who to their better natures are untrue;
Who, with palaver, strive to make black white;
Worship King Wrong;—ignore the God of right.
Gross vital-motives, and the best of fighters
For this world's goods! Your lean, high-headed writers,
With nerves and brain refined, all purely mental,—
Why, in this cat-and-dog life, are they sent all?
Mediums of thought to be; spirit to give;
To leaven matter; make it think and live;
To purge the surging mass; to deaden sin;
Lest all should stagnate and corrupt within.

While envy, slander, malice, mean and vile,
Pounce on the good, and murder with a smile.
Be ours the philosophy, my friend, to take
Things as they are; the best of life to make;
To act as if this world were not our home,
To live as if the heirs of that to come;
Where God will wipe away the sorrow-tear
That wets the good man's cheek who does his duty here.

TO W. C. T., ESQ.,

ON THE DEATH OF HIS BELOVED WIFE.

Dear Friend, be comforted! Your much-loved wife
Has passed from this into a higher life.
The pearl of your house, your Margaret's fled!
You loved her living, and you mourn her dead.
Yet nothing beautiful and good in her
Has fallen a prey to Death, the conqueror.
Then weep no more, for she exists in bliss,

In the ideal, the perfect, heaven of this.
The spirit-world (whence the immortal flows,
Source of all life from which it comes and goes)
Is round about us, not in far-off skies,
The matrix of our own in which it lies;
Whence sweet souls whisper, consolation give,
To their dear sisters here condemned to live
In earthly mansions subject to decay,
Which grow and fade and change from day to day.
Matter's immortal! how can spirit die?
Through the life-cycles, round and round we fly,
Swift as the planets round their central sun,
Until we hear God's voice exclaim, " Well done,
Thou good and faithful servant: take thy rest
In the eternal mansions of the blest!"

Life is a little cloud by the wind driven
Across the sky—a shooting star of heaven,
That flashes brightly, and then fades away,
Petty ephemera of a summer's day!
Mystery of mystery! nought understood,
As death transmutes e'en evil into good.

But oh! she's dead! and memory wakens woe.
In spite of faith and hope, my tears will flow

When on the past I gaze, her vision see,
And think how kind and good she was to me.
When stern affliction stretched me on my bed,
Crushed out my life, deprived me of my bread,
'Twas her warm heart that pitied and relieved
My wants and pain—that sympathized and grieved
At my hard lot, when summer friends showed me,
Like priest and Levite, their hypocrisy.

Best of physicians! body and soul did thrive
On her good nursing, aided by the drive
About the suburbs,—through the pulsing heart
Of the great city, in its busy mart;
Along its artery where the vessels glide,
Laden with commerce, England's wealth and pride.
She by these means gave health, assuaged my pain,
And sent me to my home a man again.

I sorrow with thee, friend; pity thy lot.
Left in thy lonely home now she is not,
You miss her footsteps on the parlour floor,
Her merry laugh, the joke that made us roar,
Her sunlight face, the music of her feet,
As down the stairs she tripped, her love to meet;

Affection's hearty kiss ; her cheerful voice
That soothed thy sorrow, caused thee to rejoice;
And the warm heart that melted when the poor
Craved for relief, and, blessing, left thy door.

Thy house is silent now ; the pretty bird
That kissed her hand and sang, the dog that heard
Her loved voice call, barked, bounded by her side,
Grew dumb, refused their food, forpined and died.
Death to the weary and afflicted, who
Pain's seven-fold heated furnace have passed through,
Is a rich blessing, sweet as is the sleep
Of a tired peasant. Then how vain to weep
That she is blest ! For though beneath the sod
Her body sleeps, her soul's awake with God.

SONNET, SONGS, AND POEMS, WRITTEN IN 1870, 1871, AND 1873.

ON THE DEATH OF A THRUSH.

THE cage is silent, Jackey! Not a note
To greet me this spring morn. What is it? Hush!
Death, the life-thief hath stolen my pretty thrush,—
Closed his bright eyes,—unstrung the tuneful throat,
Through which such floods of melody would float,
To thrill my being. Oh, how desolate
And sad I feel without my feathered mate!
Here lies his speckled body; but oh, where
Is the intelligence that soothed my care
By whistle, sign, or word? I think that death
Could not destroy it, or the vital breath;
For 'tis not magnetism, light, heat, or air,
But never-dying spirit, which doth form
And fashion matter down from man to worm.

SWEET SEVENTEEN.

Sweet seventeen!
When love is blowing
And life is flowing
   Through meadows so green,
Oh, give me life's pearl,
A dear, loving girl
   Of sweet seventeen!

Sweet seventeen!
That young May of life
When pleasure is rife,
   All morn without e'en!
Oh, give me life's pearl,
A dear, loving girl
   Of sweet seventeen!

Sweet seventeen!
The age of Elise
Just blooming to please
   Fond lover I ween!
Oh, give me life's pearl,
A dear, loving girl
   Of sweet seventeen!

Sweet seventeen!
In gossamer trim
So graceful and slim,
   With love's ardour keen!
Oh, give me life's pearl,
A dear, loving girl
   Of sweet seventeen!

Sweet seventeen!
That fountain of blisses,
Of love, and of kisses!
   How happy I've been
With life's richest pearl,
A dear, loving girl
   Of sweet seventeen!

LUCY GREEN.

I LOVED a rosy blue-eyed girl
   When I was scarce fifteen,
With luscious lips and teeth of pearl;
   Her name was Lucy Green.

It was a blessèd, joyous time:
　　Our hearts were light as feather,
As we wandered in the spring-prime
　　Within the fields together,

To cull the flowers and hear the birds
　　Their sweetest love-notes singing;
And thus I robed my thoughts in words,
　　When village bells were ringing.

"My Lucy! heaven is steeped in blue,
　　The morn her mist-veil raises,—
While angel-eyes rain pearly dew
　　On buttercups and daisies.

"The honey-bee rich nectar sips
　　From his sweet flowers in blossom;
Then, Lucy, let me taste thy lips,
　　And press thee to my bosom?

"The happy birds, the trees, and flowers,
　　All love in April weather;
The very earth and heaven in showers
　　Mingle their souls together.

"The sky stoops down to kiss the sea,
    The winds kiss flowers and grasses;
If nature kisses thus with glee,
    Why should not lads and lasses?"

ESTHER.

OH, well I remember, dear Esther,
    The time when we lovèd each other;
When we trifled, and quarrelled, and parted,
    And then became sister and brother.

Your pretty school-house which did nestle
    'Neath the Blackcap on Plumpton Down,
Where Montfort with Harry to wrestle
    Had marched through the Wealden from town.

The low, quickset hedge that surrounded
    That beautiful garden of flowers;
Where we chatted 'mid fruit trees in blossom
    At evening, and whiled away hours

In hearing the nightingale chorus
  Resounding from woodland and grove,
As night her star-mantle spread o'er us,
  ··And hymned forth the music of love.

When we wandered through wood and by hedgerow,
  All steeped in the moon's silver light,
Till the nightingale-chorus had ended,
  And dawn held the train of the night.

I married your sister, dear Esther,
  And you gave your heart to another;
Though for years you've left me and England,
  We still love—as sister and brother!

ALMENA VAUGHAN.

DIED JUNE 21, 1843.

A NOBLE, high-souled woman,
  An angel of the dawn,
A rosebud sent to bloom and die,
  Was dear Almena Vaughan!

She lay a suffering martyr,
   'Neath a snowy coverlet,
With books and flowers around her,
   On the day when first we met.

A lily-stem, wind-broken,
   At the spring of life's decline;
A lovely, fragile being,
   Who had lived a life divine!

Hers was a noble beauty,—
   The beauty of the mind:
Her brow was broad and lofty,
   Her feelings pure, refined.

Pain could not crush her spirit,
   The child of other skies!
She suffered agonies, and died,
   And is now in Paradise!

The pure and good, like violets,
   Scarce blossom at spring's dawn
Before they droop, and fade, and die,
   Like dear Almena Vaughan.

A SONG FOR THE TIMES.

AROUSE, YE MEN OF ENGLAND!

When Continental nations
   Their faith and treaties break,
Up, Spirit of Old England!
   Shake off thy sleep! awake!
A foeman's foot shall tread not
   The blessèd, hallowed soil,
Where Freedom's raised her altar,—
   Our ocean-girdled Isle.
Arouse, ye men of England!
   Let love of wealth ne'er drown
     The warlike spirit
     Which you inherit
   From sires of high renown.

The peace-at-any-price men,
   God grant they've had their day!
For they'd destroy our British pluck
   That keeps the foe away.
Then teach us, Spirit of Freedom,
   The use of gun and sword,

To guard our hearth and altar
From a ruthless foreign horde.
Arouse, ye men of England!
Let love of wealth ne'er drown
The warlike spirit
Which you inherit
From sires of high renown.

Trade, commerce, manufactures,
The tillage of the field,
Our homes, and wives, and children,
With our bodies we must shield
From the savage devastation
Of sword, of gun, and lance,
Which like a hurricane hath swept
O'er the lovely land of France.
Arouse, ye men of England!
Let love of wealth ne'er drown
The warlike spirit
Which you inherit
From sires of high renown.

This beauteous isle for ages
No foeman's foot hath trod.

And should he dare to come, he'll find
   A grave beneath her sod.
Our sires were noble freemen:
   Then shall we be less brave?
Oh, no! we'll stain our green isle red,
   Ere she shall be a slave.
Arouse, ye men of England!
   Let love of wealth ne'er drown
      The warlike spirit
      Which you inherit
   From sires of high renown.

THE POET'S LOVE-SONG.

LIKE a golden morning
   Gemmed with silver pearls,
Beauty's self adorning,
   Art thou Peer of Girls!

Cheeks like apple blossom,
   Eyes like stars of fire,
Snowy, heaving bosom,
   Rousing love's desire.

I did never meet one
   I could love like thee;
Canst thou, O my sweet one,
   Say the same to me?

As the pretty flowers
   Love the blessèd sun,
As the earth loves showers,—
   Love me, beauteous one!

As the bee loves honey.
   And the bird his song,
Or the miser money—
   I have loved thee long.

Darling, be not cruel!
   Let me round thy neck
Hang, as doth a jewel,
   Thy young life to deck.

ELISE.

Sweet is spring-time laughing
    In the month of May;
Sweet the flowers quaffing
    Dew at dawn of day;

Sweet is water flowing;
    Sweet a shady nook:
Wisdom-gems a-glowing
    In great Nature's book;

Sweet the green grass falling
    To the mower's scythe;
Sweet the cuckoo calling,
    Skylark singing blithe;

Sweet is moonlight sleeping
    On a waveless sea;
Sweet is angels' weeping
    Dewdrops on the lea;

Sweeter still at gloaming
    Voice of pretty lass;
Honey-bee a-roaming
    'Mong the waving grass;

Christine Nilsson singing
    Handel's finest tune;
Woods with music ringing
    In a night of June;

Sweet the graceful evening,
    Streaked with crimson bars;
Sweet the lovely night-veil,
    Gemmed with twinkling stars;

Sweet is pleasant weather;
    Sweet all things that please,—
Sweeter than all together
    Is beloved Elise!

A TEAR FOR THE POOR OLD MAIDS!

A TEAR for the poor old maids!
   I pity their lonely lives,
Not having been blessèd to fill
   The duties of mothers and wives.

Hurrah for the buxom wife!
   May her love-smile never fade!
She's the pride of her husband's life,
   An example to every maid!

When wives are merry and plump,
   Old maids are cross and sere;
We've a smile for the buxom wife,
   For the poor old maid a tear!

A wife's a garden of pleasure,
   A-blooming after the rain;
A maid's a miser's treasure,
   The source of nothing but pain.

Then, maid of my soul, why tarry
    For the roses of life to fade?
Oh, choose me, love me, and marry,
    Not live and die an old maid!

A tear for the poor old maids!
    I pity their lonely lives,
Not having been blessèd to fill
    The duties of mothers and wives!

THE OCEAN OF LOVE.

Oh, I am full of love
    As ocean of water;
Come and partake of it,
    Eve's fairest daughter!
Quaff of it freely,
    Lest it be hurled
Over its basin
    And re-drown the world.
Up, mighty love-wave,

Child of the tide !
    Oh, sigh on
    And fly on
To kiss your earth-bride !

As tide of the ocean
    So my love flows,
The cause of its motion
    Nobody knows.
A loving face merry
    With two brilliant eyes,
And lips like the cherry,
    Make the tide rise.
Up, mighty love-wave,
    Child of the tide !
    Oh, sigh on
    And fly on
To kiss your earth-bride !

Now you engirdle her,
    Sink in her arms,
Sweet things say to her,
    And feast on her charms.
Feed her with kisses,

And lovingly be.
Then lay at her feet
Your treasures, O sea.
Up, mighty love-wave,
Child of the tide!
Oh, sigh on
And fly on
To kiss your earth-bride!

Press her and bless her,
Ne'er from her sever,
Sing to her, love her,
And kiss her for ever!

TO MR. NAPPER.

In mind I'm often with you
Upon that summer's day
When we within the paddock
Were merry making hay.

The sea and sky were lovely,
The waves danced on the strand
Of the garden-isle of England,
That bright and beauteous land.

The pretty gabled mansion
　Embosomed 'mong the trees,
With roses round the windows,
　A-blossoming to please ;

The merry birds a-singing ;
　Thy cheerful smile, old friend ;
The sunlight-face of thy dear wife,
　To thee a real God-send.

We read the Book of Nature ;
　Turned o'er its pages sheen ;
And of the present world beheld
　Its germ, The Eocene !

Then bounded o'er the ocean,
　And viewed the Lady-Isle,
As in a golden dream she lay
　Beneath the Summer's smile.

Through rose-embowered lattice,
　I saw the dawn arise,
And strew the earth with dew-drops
　As she went up the skies,

A-steeping earth and ocean
   In floods of golden light,
While down the west horizon
   She chased the flying night.

That blissful happy visit
   Can never be forgot,
For in the desert of my life,
   'Twill be a sunny spot.

All things to me are lovely
   And sweet as sweetest briers,
In thy dear home at Bembridge,
   Earth's sweetest spot, "The Friars."

ANNIE KENT.

PRETTY little Annie Kent!
   Thou lily pure and fair,
With ruby lips and sloe-black eyes,
   Pearl-teeth and raven hair!
A little winsome wee thing,

As gentle as the dove !
A snowdrop o' the dawning year,
A morn of Spring we love !
    Little misses
    Give us blisses,
With a multitude of kisses,
    From sweet lips,
      Sweet as flowers,
    Where the bee dips
      After showers,
And the honey-dew devours !

Pretty little Annie Kent !
    Love your father, mother,
And if you've any more to spare,
    Give it to your brother.
Study, do your duty,
    Scorn vanity and pride,
Then mind and body's beauty
    Will blossom side by side.
      Up and work,
      Nor duty shirk,
But beard it bravely like a Turk ;

And a pretty
Girl that's wise,
Loving, witty,
With two eyes
Deep to gaze in as the skies!

Pretty little Annie Kent!
Death hath been and reft us
Of a loved one,* good and true,
Then in sorrow left us!
Let us weep no more, but smile,—
His shade is hov'ring o'er us!
He's only gone a little while
To Spirit-Land before us!
We shall meet him
There, and greet him,—
When attacked by Death defeat him!
Rise in air,
As sweet perfume
Of roses rare
When in bloom,
And escape the body's doom!

---

* Richard Howell, her grandfather, who died suddenly, March 18th, 1871.

AMY.

I SIT upon the cliff above the strand,
    Sighing for thee :
And see thee walking on the silver sand,
    By the calm sea,

Whose dancing wavelets playfully salute
    Thy tiny feet,
And woo thee with a love-song never mute—
    Soft, low, and sweet.

The saucy breezes, flying from the south—
    Beams of the sun—
Play with thy tresses, kiss thy cheeks and mouth,
    Belovèd one !

Oh, would I were a wave of yon blue sea,
    Sunbeam, or breeze,
That I might give sweet kisses unto thee—
    Kisses that please.

Free are thy auburn tresses, and not wedded
    To that device
Which makes a lovely woman double-headed—
    Ugly as vice !

Oh, never should a graceful angel-form
    Be fashion's ban :
Seeking to show descent up from the worm,
    Fish, monkey, man !

Putting aside the wise man's absurd whim,
    Sweet maiden, I
Firmly believe thou cam'st from cherubim
    In yonder sky.

Divine thou art—of origin divine—
    And walk'st the earth
In majesty and beauty : a pure sign
    Of heavenly birth.

Turn hitherward thy steps, and leave the sea
    Sated with kisses ;
Come to this flowery bank, and sit by me,
    Thirsting for blisses !

Oh, tell me, maiden of the lofty brow,
    'Neath which thought dwells ;
What makes both bud and leaf burst from the bough,
    Life from its cells ?

And thoughts, like lightning, flashing from thine eyes,
    To words give birth?
And beautify thy face as stars the skies,
    And flowers the earth?

What makes the pretty birds for music thirst
    On leaf and spray?
Sing to their mates, as if their hearts would burst,
    By night and day?

Enamels leaf and flower of every hue,—
    Makes sea and sky
Assume a lovelier, a diviner blue,
    And mortals sigh

For sweet companionship—woman for man,
    And dove for dove?
Oh, solve the mystery, maiden, if you can?
    What is it?—Love?

MAY-SONG.

'Tis the merry month of May!
    Mother-earth is fresh and green,
Bud and leaf are on the spray,
    Beauty everywhere is seen!
Buds are here—flowers are there—
Gemming earth, perfuming air:
Primrose, cowslip, violet,
    Hawthorn, buttercup, and sloe,
Forget-me-not, maiden's pet
    Sweet May-lily, white as snow.
But, sweet roses, poets say
Ye blossom in the month o' May;
I do seek ye in parterre,
Field and hedgerow—everywhere.
Poets, this is merry May!
Earth her garland now discloses—
    Flowers are there,
    Of beauty rare—
But I look in vain for roses!

In the merry month of May,
    Roses sweet are blossoming:

Thus the Grecian poets say,
  And you copy what they sing.
But, in England, chant the tune,
  Roses blow in sunny June !
Though the May-month has no roses
  'Tis the sweetest of the year :
Earth her jewel-case uncloses—
  Beauteous life-forms then appear.
Insects, steeped in gorgeous dyes,
Fill the earth and wing the skies.
Life below and life above—
May is full of joy and love !
Poets, this is merry May !
Earth her garland now discloses—
    Flowers are there,
    Of beauty rare—
But I look in vain for roses !

In the merry month of May,
  Loving season of the spring,
Merry birds sing night and day,
  In the bushes, on the wing.
Floods of music everywhere,
Rise with incense in the air :

Hear the white-throat, black-cap, thrush,
  Sweetly warbling in the vale!
But the king-bird sings, and, hush!
  All are mute to hear his tale.
Rose and nightingale!—sweet words:
Queen o' flowers and king o' birds!
One I hear, in merry May,
Warble love-songs night and day;
But the queen of roses fair,
I do seek her everywhere.
Poets, this is merry May!
Earth her garland now discloses—
    Flowers are there,
    Of beauty rare—
But I look in vain for roses!

A WALKING BAROMETER.

TO MY ESTEEMED FRIEND, J. J. SEWELL, ESQ.

Oh, why does life's essence,
  The beautiful rain,
Give mother-earth pleasure,
  And my body pain?

I'm a walking barometer,
  Ruled by the weather,
With spirits lead-heavy,
  Or light as a feather !
    Rain, rain!
    Wind, snow, and rain !
    Why at your coming
    Do you give me pain ?

On a beautiful day,
  Be I peevish and low,
'Tis a sign that a cutting
  North-easter will blow.
And should I be maddened,
  Or groaning with pain,
In a very few hours
  Down tumbles the rain.
    Rain, rain !
    Thunder and rain !
    Why at your coming
    Do you give me pain ?

This essence of life,
  Which over earth flows,

Its coming and going,
  Why, nobody knows!
Life is a mystery,
  All blended in one;
That flows like a stream,
  Into earth from the sun.
    Rain, rain!
    Mist, fog, and rain!
      Why at your coming
      Do you give me pain?

Philosophers think,
  And orators chatter,
On body and mind,
  On spirit and matter.
Chop logic to prove,
  By dogmatic rules,
Mind's only brain-action,—
  And prove themselves fools.
    Rain, rain!
    Frost, hail, and rain!
      Why at your coming
      Do you give me pain?

What dunces we are,
    Though proud o' the knowledge
We've gained by self-teaching,
    Or cramming at College.
O' the weather, experience
    Has taught I'm the tool,
And I've just enough wisdom
    To know I'm a fool!
        Rain, rain!
    Wind, snow, and rain!
    Why at your coming
    Do you give me pain?

EPITAPH.

HERE lies a pretty baby,
    A snowdrop without stain!
Who left the spirit-world of bliss
To dwell but thirteen months in this,
    And then went back again.

Blossom o' forget-me-not,
　　Daisy pearled by rain,
A pretty lamb, a wee nestling,
With downy fluff upon its wing,
　　Ideal of poet's brain!

She came here with the flowers,
　　Sweetbrier, mignonette,
When the glad voice of fairy Spring
Her sweetest songs to heaven did sing,
　　To wear life's coronet.

But when a second summer
　　Arrayed herself in pride,
God's angel came and gave his sting.
But ere the soul assumed its wing,
　　She looked up, smiled, and died.

Green grass and flowers adorn
　　The grave where baby lies.
When I recall her tiny form,
So full of life, now prey of worm,
　　Big tear-drops blind my eyes.

Oh little precious baby,
A snowdrop without stain !
Who left the spirit-world of bliss
To dwell but thirteen months in this,
And then went back again.

WAIF THOUGHTS.

COMPOSED ON A BED OF SICKNESS, INSCRIBED TO

J. J. SEWELL, ESQ.

1873.

A FRIEND, dear Sewell, is a friend in need,
And such to me thou'st proved by word and deed.
A good physician, and of matchless skill,
Thou find'st a remedy for many an ill
That flesh is heir to in this mortal life,
Whose origin sets philosophers at strife,
Who, knowing nothing, ask and answer queries,—

Write books about it, crammed brimful of theories,
And show their learning but amounts to this,
That life is life, and will remain what 'tis.
Quivering with pain and gasping for my breath,
Trembling I lay before the spirit, Death,
Willing to cross the threshold of his portal,
Into the promise-land of souls immortal;
Stricken with awe, and peering through the gloom,
And fearfully wondering what would be my doom
Till my eyes closed in agonies of pain,
And all the world of life did from me wane.
Was it a new life? was I in a trance?
When Death and thou arose upon my glance,
Contending for my body, seeming dead,
Yet still attached to life by one small thread.
Thou didst prevail,—I shivered, sighed, drew breath,
And heard these words fall from the lips of Death:
"Thy boldness and thy skill deserve reward.
There lies the prize, a poor unhappy bard;
I'll wait a little longer for my prey."
Then with a gentle smile he went his way.

    Why, as God's agent, did you spare me, friend?
The Vicar tells me for some useful end.
And though I have my doubts, yet still I'll try

To do a little good before I die.
Ay! e'en tho' haunted by the grim and gaunt
Forerunner of starvation, cruel Want!
Who with his wolfish eyes glares in my face,
And hugs me, bear-like, in his foul embrace;
Then gnaws me to the bone, hyena-like;
Asks Death to slay me, yet he will not strike,
Strike the fell blow, sharp as the woodman's stroke
That topples to the ground the giant-oak.
   Oh why, my friend, should poverty e'er cling
As ivy to the tree to those that sing,
Stealing the nourishment which God doth give
To all His sons that they may eat and live?
Is it that suffering should prepare them here
For their translation to a better sphere?
As that good Book, the Christian's hope and trust,
Says, God loves those He humbles to the dust.
   Though stricken by affliction, poor as Job,
Low my position, and no costly robe
Adorn my body,—made the scoff and scorn
Of purse-proud men,—destitute, forlorn,—
Yet God, in compensations ever kind,
To my weak body's given a strong mind;
Active in age as in the days of youth,

In study, observation, seeking truth.
Great Nature's book near fifty years I've studied,
Yet is my reason blown? Nay, scarcely budded!
Little I know of Nature's vast expanse,
Although I've learned to know my ignorance.
The more I learn, yet still the more I see,
I've got no farther than my A B C.

While life remains, dear friend, still let us find
Something t' instruct and cultivate the mind;
Let's glean a little of the wondrous plan
Of this life-world from monad up to man;
Whose many contradictions make it seem
Confusion worse confounded, a wild dream.
But 'tis our ignorance that make us see
Things out of joint, that are in harmony;
Perfect in part, perfection in the whole,
Though seen imperfect by the human soul.
Dimly we gaze on all, through a smoked glass,
See but in part, distinguish not the mass;
Yet dare to criticise, as strange and odd,
The perfect works of the all-perfect God!

These robes in which our spirits are arrayed
Belong to matter, of which earth is made.
Hourly we put on flesh, hourly it goes.

Resembling ocean, in its ebbs and flows.
Yesterday 'twas mine; 'tis yours to-day;
Pervading life-forms in a different way.
To-day in grass, to-morrow beast, and then
As nourishment, it passes into men;
Around the matter goes in cycles, friend,
Like earth, without beginning, without end.
In nature thus we see, as through a glass,
That great prophetic truth, "all flesh is grass."
 But mark another wonder, great and strange,
Throughout the phases of the body's change,
The beauteous soul, the vivifying flame,
Amid the wreck of matter's still the same.
The same that seized th' elements and designed,
And built a body for herself and mind,
To play their parts in on this earthly stage,
From youth to manhood, manhood to old age.
While through the phases that intervene,
The memory of her acts is ever green;—
This living memory of every act
From birth to death to me's a proven fact
That the blest soul's immortal! Sweet to me
Are the remembrances of infancy,
Of youth and manhood. Sweet to think upon

God's noblemen like Frederick Robertson!
Teaching great truths unto his brother-men
From pulpit and from platform! Toilers then
Extracted honey from his lips, as bees
Did from the honeyed lips of Sophocles.
And how they loved him! how they grieved the day
They saw his loved remains consigned to clay!
Though twenty years have passed, yet have they not
Of all he did for them the least forgot;
He and his deeds, still in their memories bloom
Sweet as the flowers they rear around his tomb!

———o———

www.ingramcontent.com/pod-product-compliance
Lightning Source LLC
Chambersburg PA
CBHW031816220426
43662CB00007B/675